Black Men
WHO HAVE MADE
A DIFFERENCE

MINNIE L. RANSOM ED. D.

ISBN: 978-1-64314-818-2 (Paperback)
        978-1-64314-819-9 (Hardback)
        978-1-64314-820-5 (E-book)

Library of Congress Control Number: 2023907031

AuthorsPress
California, USA
www.authorspress.com

Special Dedication to my Grandchildren, Kaliah,
Daelen, De'jan, Siobhan, Kaliese,
and all children of the world.

Black Men Who Have Made A Difference

by Minnie L. Ransom, Ed.D.

book review by Jonah Meyer

Taken as a whole, there is much within these pages for readers to enjoy—and much material, undoubtedly, from which one can learn about important work by black men in America, impressively spanning from the early 1730s to the present day.

— Jonah Meyer
The US Review of Books

Black Men Who Have Made A Difference
by Minnie L. Ransom, Ed.D.

"Become with hard work and a prayer, doctors, lawyers, scientists, astronauts, authors, poets, educators, inventers, innovators, creators, artists, athletes, actors, or whatever your heart desires."

Ransom bookends her tome on black men in America who have made a positive impact on the lives of all Americans, both historically and at present, with original poetry at the beginning and end. Her words call upon readers to "Respect Yourself and Others," and then, "Chase Your Dreams." "Have hope for the future which is essential. And live up to your full potential," the educator advises in the first while insisting in the latter that one "Stand up for what is fair and right. It does not matter your height. Have empathy, sympathy, and compassion for others. In God's eyes, we should treat each other as brothers."

The real substance of the book consists of the nearly 150 pages in between, where a range of black men's lives and their unique contributions to our society and world are examined and celebrated, each individual occupying his own chapter, complete with basic biographical information and specifics of their differing significant causes and outstanding impacts on society. Ransom includes such diverse individuals as George Floyd, Tyler Perry, Barack Obama, Stephen Harvey, John Carlos, Muhammad Ali, Emmett Till, John Lewis, Martin Luther King, Jr., Malcolm X, Jackie Robinson, Jessie Owens, Thurgood Marshall, Dr. Charles Richard Drew, Dr. Ralph Bunche, Dick Rowland, George Washington Carver, Booker T. Washington, Elijah McCoy, Nat Turner, Fredrick Douglas, Benjamin Banneker, and too many more to mention in this space. Doctors and inventors, politicians and sports heroes alike, all of the people whose life stories are encapsulated in this marvelous collection share the following in common: they are male, they are black, and, despite harrowing societal conditions and, in many of these cases, either being born into slavery or only one or two generations removed from such, they each in their own way rose to the top of their respective fields and made an absolute difference for the better, for all.

Ransom, it seems, was born to write this book. Her scholarship on the subject and the apparent passion the author is guided by in selecting and sharing the inspiring stories of these men shine through on each page, from beginning to end. Each chapter (and thus, each featured individual) includes artwork and photography to further illustrate and place into perspective the lives of these individuals. Further, at the end of the work of biographical and historical nonfiction, a selection of full-color photographs of the author and her husband (aka Papa Joe), family, and friends showcases in endearing terms the couple's social group (such as one taken on a Bay cruise), travel throughout the country with family and fellow RV group members, and participation in barbeque cook-off competitions. This personalization of the author and her family, at the book's end, serves as a nice touch, both visually and in terms of rounding out a bit more about the book's creator. Taken as a whole, there is much within these pages for readers to enjoy—and much material, undoubtedly, from which one can learn about important work by black men in America, impressively spanning from the early 1730s to the present day.

book review by Jonah Meyer

US Review of Books

Contents

Respect Yourself and Others

By: Minnie L. Ransom ED. D.

Show respect for yourself, others, and their differences:
You never know the consequences.

Have hope for the future which is essential:
And live up to your full potential.

Be a part of change for the better:
Many dreams potentially not to shatter.
Being true to yourself is what really matters.

Accept defeat with grace and know:
That everything presents a lesson to grow.
Never give up even when doors are closed although:
You stood for what was right: Someday your blessings will overflow.

Slangs, vulgar, and obscene language is not a part of your vocabulary.
You are smart and can use many other words from the dictionary.

Pull up those pants: Be proud, not shy:
Like the proud people you are, holding your head high.
Walk tall as if your heads were being pulled to the sky.

Sit up in your chair.
There is no time to spare.

Sit at the front of the class, sitting in the back has long passed.
Not distracting or being distracted by others.
Focus! Be in the present; One place and not head is in another.
Participate. Really listen; Take it in.
Learning is not a sin! Learning starts from within.
Learn all that is presented to you from class beginning to end.

Leave those fears and negativities behind you.
Of which there are a few.
Being called Nerd, Teacher's Pet, Show-Off, or even a Geek.
Do not let these make you weak.

You may even be accused of trying to be more than who you are:
You will not let that stop you from being a star.
Even when asked if you think you are better than the rest:
You know for you what is best.

All of this in not a coincidence.
Snuffling out your light burning bright:
With all their might:
May make theirs begin to flicker.
They may think that they are slicker.
Being all that you can be is demonstrating your true existence!
To not show your brilliance is to be nonexistence!

Black Men Who Have Made a Difference
George Perry Floyd Jr. (1973 – 2020)

George Floyd was born on October 14, 1973,
in Fayetteville, North Carolina with siblings 3.
His Great, Great, Grandfather was a slave,
A free man at 8 years old was his age.
He bought land with money he saved.
Settlers stole his land to him no one gave.

At a young age George was always stopped and searched,
on the way to school, to the store, or even to church.
Always a suspect by the police and always harassed.
For his friends and him survival was to not talk about
the police brutality,
And systematic racism that they saw or had to endure,
in their neighborhood without any kindness or morality.
George was always in survival mode, hard worker, poor,
funny, loved Football, and in a racist world learned to endure.
He was smart, intergenic, athletic, and loved basketball.
He was generous, kindhearted, loved his mother most of all.
He inspired to play basketball professionally.
Saw athletics as the way out of the ghetto personally.

He relocated to Texas, however, being poor,
still could only live in the city poverty core.
in Florida, without the education required,
he could not survive college and could only get jobs undesired.

He soon went back to Texas where he got his first felony,
for selling a minor quantity of drugs, he was taken into custody.
Later the system failed him in getting back on his feet.
He started to be devoured by the fines, and not able to get work,
no assistance anywhere. Hard worker not able to prove his worth.
He soon got into difficulties once again,
selling small amounts of drugs for henchmen.
No other way to make money, he made wrong choices,
that caused him to continue to down spiral in charges,
of continuing to sell small amounts of drugs.
Some charges were believed to be fabricated by the police.
Regardless, for him there was no relief or release.
Despite his personal struggles, he commanded
a lot of admiration.
He kept a good reputation in his community;
he advised young men, there were many;
and he got involved with a church ministry.
He transformed himself into a position of a role model type,
conversing with others about the unpleasant elements of life.
While also encouraging them to try and overcome their strife;
to figure out ways to prevail, despite their fights.

George met Pastor Riles who thought that he wanted a reform.
He suggested that George leave Houston and go to a nine-month
platform.
A change in atmosphere, clean slate, a new beginning,
a fresh emphasis.
It taught work skills and had some rehabilitation services
at the Salvation Army in Minneapolis it taught life practices.
The program was completely inclusive
and the people there would be receptive.

Being the football fan he was, George was persuaded to go
to the place for his life to unfold.
He decided that the Super Bowl was the faith to have his
change of life decided.
The Super Bowl LI, the New England Patriots and the Atlanta
Falcons, was played in Houston that year.
It would be played in Minnesota the next year.
George was going to follow the Super Bowl he concluded.

The Sunday after the Super Bowl in Houston, he got on a bus
And went to Minneapolis.
He arrived in Minneapolis in February of 2017,
For his future he hoped for the best, but it was all unforeseen.
However, his life he needed to intervene.
He was hopeful that moving to Minneapolis was
a positive change.
The treatment center was one of the few treatment centers
specifically geared toward Black people.
For a better life, he was willing to make a chance.
There he started opening up.
He was disappointed that he never became
a professional athlete,
He was hiding his feelings beneath.
In his 40s, with children of his own,
he was looking for answers and a sense of reason.
If sports were not going to define his future,
how would his life be of service?

For a change, things started going well for him,
and he was excited about his progress.
His family back home he would not forget.
He got a security job, at the Salvation Army and to offset
his income, he added another job at a Latin nightclub.
The owner of the nightclub owned rental properties
around Minneapolis and he rented one to George.

A nice townhome in an elegant part of town.
It was near a lot of big, expensive, single-family homes
overlooking sparkling waters with nice bones.
For the first time, George was living
in the White part of town.
He had a roommate named, Big E. that he had
met at the center.
A big man, like George, but warm and tender.
He told his friends that he had never encountered police
officers like the ones in that neighborhood before,
quite unique!
They smiled and waved at him. It felt very weird to him,
in disbelief.

One day Floyd came home to find that Big E. his friend
had overdosed and was dead.
For this it was hard for him to attend.
Even though he later got two more roommates.
He was never the same. He was in a state.
It seemed that every time he started to take a step
toward a life he wanted, something would happen
and backward he would be swept.
Thinking that, his brother was a truck driver,
he could do that too. It would have helped
him to get financially stable, motivate him higher
giving some financial freedom to help improve his life,
and to also improve the life of his family back home.

He tried to take the tests for the permit.
He could not get the permit because he owed
fees back in Texas.
These fees the state would not release.
He could not finish all the training to get the complete
commercial driver's license because he had to work.
At work, hours were set and there were no perks.

He could not find a regular 9:00-to-5:00 job that would allow
him to work and then go to get his trucking license,
because of his arrest record he was not without.
The only jobs that would give George a chance were the jobs
that looked at his size they would want a Black man for toiling hard,
like jobs lifting heavy things, intimidating people, nightclub jobs
kicking people out, or a bodyguard.
The night jobs would leave him tired in the day, prohibiting
his ability to be able to get the truck driver's license.
He also owed child support for kids back home.
Nothing he could do for truck driving school was positioning
him to be able to better his life.
A half-year after Big E dies, George got a phone call,
his mother had also died.
George was starting to be up against a wall.
Living in Minneapolis, he prided himself on being still,
the man of that house in Houston, hard shoes to fill.
He was the oldest son, and he was known
to send money and clothes back home.
He now had to take care of and play a bigger role
in raising the grandchildren that his mother had prior control.

He would be heard in his room reading Bible verses and crying.
Life did not get easier for him, not in the lack of trying.
Regardless of how he tried to display preservation
his friends from the center's perception
was that he had started to display serious signs of depression.

Friends from the program at the center with him knew additions
of persistent possibilities of death, the feelings of uncertainties,
the economic instabilities, were a person's prime conditions
to begin to relapse or to increase their drug dependencies.

George was said to have bought cigarettes on May 25, 2020
with a counterfeit $20 bill.
Seventeen minutes after the first squad car arrived at the scene,
George was unconscious and pinned beneath three police officers,
Showing no signs of life. He was killed over a $20 bill.
Instead of going to jail, he would be going to a coroner.
Combining videos from bystanders and security cameras
viewed from the corner of businesses
all agreed that George was a Black man that all witnesses saw
murdered by a police during what was supposed to be
an arrest even after George said he could not breathe.

Derek Chauvin, one of four police officers who arrived
on the scene, knelt on George's neck and back for 9 minutes
and 29 seconds in plain sight.
His actions were clearly seen by all that he violated
human rights.
Ignoring human rights and the policies of the Minneapolis Police
Department, he left George unable to breathe, even
George and onlookers repeatedly called for him to cease.

He did not remove his knee even after George lost consciousness
and for a full minute and 20 seconds after paramedics
The world saw Derek Chauvin's behavior arriving on the scene.
It was only befitting that the world would see
the prolonged consequences.

Video footage was seen on national TV.
His trial was televised live on national TV for the world to see.
Beginning on March 8, 2021, and concluded on April 20, 2021,
he was charged with second-degree/third-degree murder,
and second-degree manslaughter.

Finally fellow officers are taking the right side of justice,
testifying against corrupt officers like Derek Chauvin
and telling the truth.
He was found guilty of all charges.

On March 12, Minneapolis agreed to pay $27 million
to settle George's family's wrongful death lawsuit.
Changing laws in his name, the family is continuing to pursue.

On June 25, 2021, Chauvin was sentenced to 22.5 years
for second-degree murder.
The sentencing is not what some wanted but it is a beginning
to securing justice for all people.

Many Black men and their families have come face to face,
with the forces of systemic racism like George Floyd
did on that fatal day.

Even during the 21st century other Black Americans have confronted,
systematic racism in America only because of their skin
color in one way or another since slavery.

Their true freedom and democracy by some were never really wanted.
Causes of this deep-rooted automatic hatred of humans,
just because of the color of their skin has carried overwhelmingly,
Over to some in authority believing they could do whatever they
want systemically.

Brutalizing, killing, covering up, and hiding behind their badges of
protection,
going unpunished and unharmed, never bothered about subjection.
Years of toxic societal behavior and treatment remaining uncorrected,
negatively shaping Black peoples' behavior and experiences, socially,
personally, and professionally over the course of more than a century.

Times have changed slowly but there is still a lot left to do.
We still have a long way to go for all to make the Constitution true.
Some young Blacks had become assimilated,
felt that their lives were different from their parents' affiliated.
Only to have a rude awakening by those demonstrating,
later their true colors and hatred for them as Black people.
Too many young Black men have been slain, locked up,
in one way or another without justice for their deaths
or incarceration,
observed or concealed always allowing the law officers' word
to be taken over the observers in cases of racist and corrupt police.
Privilege, fame, education, nor economic status,
never being a factor to keep Black people safe,
out in a world with hatred inter woven within like a lattice;
Black parents always terrified for their children and themselves,
being stopped by the police, knowing like others, never in parallel.
Never able to prove their cases or obtain justice,
from those who pulled ranks and couldn't be trusted;
Settled with trying to keep themselves and others from the injustice.

The handy invention of a small multi use devise,
carried by young and old, rich and poor, using it, do not think twice.
found its way into nearly all Americans' possession,
the cell phones with video camera used in all professions,
turned out to be reliable witnesses that could not be denied.

One summer, Black parents who always feared for their children,
in a world killed by the thousand but no one listen,
along with others, all races and creeds came to protest,
locally, nationwide, and in over 60 countries in the flesh.
The openly killing of a poor Black man,
bringing to justice those who took his life in their own hands.

Protesting is what they knew best,
demonstrating that his killing was not deserved for an arrest.
For once, out of all the past concealed beatings and killings,
of thousands of Black men near and far without any feelings,
caught the attention of those held hostage by the
Covid 19 Pandemic.
They thought enough to speak up, stand up, to shed light on
wrongs, a problem gigantic.

In the right place and time, finally for others to really listen.
The world helped tremendously to get justice for that wrong
in the past that had been hidden.
This one incident clearly racist and outright hatred driven.
With hope for the future that all human lives will finally
be of significance.

George Floyd

https://www.loc.gov/pictures/item/2020638181/

George Floyd
https://www.loc.gov/pictures/resource/vrg.13649/

Tyler Perry (1969 –)

Tyler Perry, born Emmitt Perry Jr in 1969, the 13th of September.
Born in New Orleans, Louisiana. His father was a carpenter.
He has three siblings and, in the household, his father
was the oppressor.
As a child, Tyler once went so far as to attempt suicide
to escape beatings from his father.
He realized a unique sanctuary and satisfaction unlike no other,
when he attended church services each week with his mother.

At age 16, he had his first name legally changed
from Emmitt to Tyler to distance himself from his father's chains.

Many years later, after seeing the film "*Precious*",
he was moved to reveal behavior of others noxious
for the first time, at the precious age of ten
he had been molested by the mother of a friend.

He was also molested prior by three men.
Later he learned his own father had molested his friend.
A DNA test taken by Tyler indicated that Emmitt Sr.
was not his biological father creature.

Tyler did not complete high school. He earned a GED.
In his early 20s, watching an episode of *Oprah Winfrey*,
he heard someone describe the act of writing,
having effects on the author being therapeutic,
enabling him or her to work out problems better than anesthetic.
This comment inspired Tyler to apply himself to a career in writing.
Soon he was writing a series of letters to himself that became,
the basis for the musical ***I Know I've Been Changed***.

Around 1990, Tyler moved to Atlanta. Two years, later
at a community theater financed by then Tyler, even braver
his musical, *I Know I've Been Changed* was first performed.
The 22-year-old Tyler with his $12,000 life savings,
financed the play that was a financial failure.
Tyler persisted and rewrote,
the play over the next six years. It was his pen that spoke.

He succeeded in restaging his play in Atlanta in 1998.
He continued to create new stage productions at age 28.
Touring with his plays, he started to develop loyal supporters
in size that was great.

In 2005 it was reported that he had sold "in tickets more than
$100 million.
He was getting his stories out and to his heart, he listen.
Tyler was estimated to have sold in video sales of his shows
$30 million.
He was also estimated to have sold in merchandise $20 million.

The 300 live shows Tyler produces each year are attended by an
average of 35,000 people a week.
He is an American actor, director, producer, and screenwriter.
His life is no longer hard or bleak.
He has written, produced, and stared in many films.
Writing stage plays also continues to be a gift for him.

He is said to be worth more than 1 billion dollars.
He turned his life around and decided to be a winner.
Tyler has developed several television series
writing to his own satisfaction, with no one to appease.

On October 2, 2012, he struck an exclusive multi-year
partnership with Oprah Winfrey and her network.
Based on his previous success, he was to bring

scripted television to the network.
The partnership turns out to be a huge display of successful teamwork.
Tyler has created multiple scripted series for the network,
that have been very profitable, giving the network its ratings highest,
biggest success story, and the partnership for both the sweetest.

In 2015, Tyler acquired the 330-acre former military base
located in Atlanta without a debt or delays.
He converted it into studios with standing permanent sets,
a mock cheap hotel, a real 1950s-style diner, a trailer park set,
a mansion, a replica of a luxury hotel lobby,
and best White House replica yet.

It also has 12 sound stages named after highly accomplished Black
Americans in the entertainment industry.
On February 19, 2018, Tyler announced enthusiastically,
that on one of the new stages that was a hit instantly,
the movie, *Black Panther*, which was the first to be videoed.
Tyler Perry Studios is one of the largest in the nation film studios
with all around talent hitting the country like volcanos.

He has come a long way from his troubled beginnings.
Hollywood is not the only place for film recordings.
Tyler is reaping the benefits of his labor.
He is the first Black to outright own a studio so major.

President Barack Hussein Obama II (1961 –)

Barack was born in Honolulu, Hawaii.
His mother was from Kansas, his father from Kenya.
They had generosity learned in their Midwestern tenure.
Barack was raised with his grandparents' assistance,
teaching him to hold values and obligations highly.
He had compassion, always showed mercy, and empathy.
He would devote his life to giving every child a chance to enjoy
some of life's splendor.
He didn't believe that children's fundamental rights
should be hindered.
He wanted them all to have the same chance America gave
him for his life endeavor.

He attended Chicago public schools.
Between his family and school developing all the right tools.
He has an innate sense of optimism,
Always looking on the brighter side without radicalism.

He worked his way through college with the help of scholarships.
The aide of student loans helped to lighten the hardship.
In law school, he became the first Black American president
of the Harvard Law Review.
All could see that he had true virtue.

When he returned to Illinois he began a career in public service,
taught constitutional law and became a civil right attorney.
In Chicago he worked as an organizer in the community.

For the public a trusty servant he stood seriously.
He graduated in 1983 from Columbia University.
At the University of Chicago from 1992 to 2004
he shared his virtuosity.

Barack helped by working with a group of churches.
He labored with the people in the trenches.
He worked with churches near the local closed steel plants.
He could see that they needed help at a glance.
He helped to rebuild communities devastated by the closures.
On him they could rely and he would be a strong shoulder.

The experience perfected his belief in the power of uniting.
In the hard work of citizenship, ordinary people were convincing.
Around a purpose people could bring about positive change merging.

He met the love of his life, Michelle Robinson who studied sociology
and African-American studies at Princeton University.
After graduating from Harvard Law School in Chicago she worked
at a firm called, Sidley & Austin, where she later met Barack,
the man who would become the love of her life.

They married and had two beautiful, intelligent, and
well-behaved daughters.
Seeing them together, anyone could sense the bond and love
between them, a true family role model to follow.
They each had a true calling, working the blessings
from above with people, to serve their communities,
and their neighbors demonstrating true love.

He represented the 13th district in the Illinois Senate from
1997 until 2004,
when he ran for the U.S. Senate floor.
Barack received national attention in 2004
with his March Senate primary win proving
for him there was so much more.

His well-received July Democratic National Convention
keynote address also would have many repeating his quotations.
In 2008, he was nominated by the Democratic Party
for president a year after beginning his campaign.
Barack was elected over Republican nominee John McCain.
after a close primary against Hillary Clinton campaign.

In the general election he became the country's leader.
He was a great president and a very eloquent speaker.
Serving as the 44th president and the first Black president
of the United States from 2009 to 2017
with talents for some were unforeseen.

He was inaugurated alongside his running mate, Joe Biden,
on January 20, 2009. Nine months later,
he was named the Nobel Peace Prize laureate in 2009.
Many landmark bills into law during his first two years
in office President Obama signed.

During his second term to the Supreme Court, he nominated
three justices.
For gun control he would advocate fearless.
He supported inclusion acts; issued wide-ranging executive actions
that were concerning global warming and immigration.
During President Obama's terms in office, the United States' reputation
abroad, as well as the American economy, improved significantly.
Even after he left office, President Obama's presidency generally
has continued to be frequently regarded favorably.
Among historians, political scientists' evaluations,
and the general public he is placed among the upper tier of
American presidents.

President Obama, his wife, Michelle, Joe, and Jill Biden in times
of great challenges and changes had steep hills to climb.
For the American people they made a difference in their lives.

Under President Obama's leadership a stronger economy
was ushered in, a more equal society,
a nation more secure at home and created more respected
around the world.

Many have stated that if he could have run again,
they would have voted for him.
There was not the divisiveness; disrespect of;
true lace of or caring to abide by the law;
lack of caring for, or respect of human rights
as in the Trump era that followed.

Although there were times when some would try
to find ways to slander.
On his family, they could not put a damper.
Barack with Michelle, as First Lady, by his side
continued to love each other and their family.
They actively did for them what came naturally.
They continued their efforts to support, inspire
young people, and the world achieving their desire.

The Obama years were ones in which more people
began to see themselves in the changing face of America,
to see America the way he always had, as the only place on Earth
where so many American stories could even be possible.

Barack is an accomplished author of books from 1995 – 2021
Speaking to his optimism, a few of his book titles are:
Dreams From My Father; A Promised Land; Of Thee I Sing;
The Audacity of Hope: Barack Obama Speeches;
and *Thoughts on Reclaiming the American Dream.*

> *"True democracy is a project that's much bigger than any one*
> *of us. It's bigger than any one person, any one president, and*
> *any one government. It's a job for all of us."*

President Barack Obama (2ⁿᵈ Term)
https://www.loc.gov/pictures/resource/ppbd.00603/

President Barack Obama (1ˢᵗ Term)
https://www.loc.gov/pictures/resource/ppbd.00358/

Barack Obama's campaign slogan for the first term.

OFFICIAL BALLOT
ALAMEDA COUNTY, CALIFORNIA
NOVEMBER 4, 2008 GENERAL ELECTION

INSTRUCTIONS TO VOTERS: USE BLACK OR BLUE BALLPOINT PEN ONLY. To vote for a candidate of your choice, complete the arrow ← to the right of the candidate's name. To vote for a qualified write-in candidate, PRINT the person's name in the blank space provided and complete the arrow. To vote on any measure, complete the arrow after the word "Yes" or "No."

VOTER DETACH AND KEEP THIS STUB
ALAMEDA COUNTY, CALIFORNIA
NOVEMBER 4, 2008 GENERAL ELECTION

#4
821500
BT: 160

PRESIDENT OF THE UNITED STATES

PRESIDENT AND VICE PRESIDENT

Vote for One Party

CYNTHIA MCKINNEY — for President
ROSA CLEMENTE — for Vice President — GREEN

ALAN KEYES — for President
WILEY S. DRAKE, SR. — for Vice President — AMERICAN INDEPENDENT

RALPH NADER — for President
MATT GONZALEZ — for Vice President — PEACE AND FREEDOM

BARACK OBAMA — for President
JOE BIDEN — for Vice President — DEMOCRATIC

BOB BARR — for President
WAYNE A. ROOT — for Vice President — LIBERTARIAN

JOHN MCCAIN — for President
SARAH PALIN — for Vice President — REPUBLICAN

UNITED STATES REPRESENTATIVE

13TH CONGRESSIONAL DISTRICT

SCHOOL

NEW HAVEN UNIFIED SCHOOL DISTRICT GOVERNING BOARD MEMBERS

Vote for no more than Three

MICHELLE PARNALA MATTHEWS — Parent/Youth Mentor
KEVIN HARPER — Incumbent
JONAS DINO — Incumbent
KAREN M. YIFRU — Parent/Business Analyst
SARABJIT KAUR CHEEMA — Engineer/Teacher/Parent

CITY OF UNION CITY

FOR MAYOR

Vote for One

MARK GREEN — Mayor

FOR MEMBER OF CITY COUNCIL

Vote for One

JIM NAVARRO — Incumbent

DISTRICT

ALAMEDA COUNTY WATER DISTRICT DIRECTORS

Vote for no more than Three

MEASURES SUBMITTED TO THE VOTERS

STATE

1A SAFE, RELIABLE HIGH-SPEED PASSENGER TRAIN BOND ACT. To provide Californians a safe, convenient, affordable, and reliable alternative to driving and high gas prices; to provide good-paying jobs and improve California's economy while reducing air pollution, global warming greenhouse gases, and our dependence on foreign oil, shall $9.95 billion in bonds be issued to establish a clean, efficient high-speed train service linking Southern California, the Sacramento/San Joaquin Valley, and the San Francisco Bay Area, with at least 90 percent of bond funds spent for specific projects, with private and public matching funds required, including, but not limited to, federal funds, funds from revenue bonds, and local funds, and all bond funds subject to independent audit? Fiscal Impact: State costs of $19.4 billion, assuming 30 years to pay both principal and interest costs of the bonds. Payments would average about $647 million per year. When constructed, unknown operation and maintenance costs, probably over $1 billion annually, at least partially, and potentially fully, offset by passenger fares.

YES
NO

2 STANDARDS FOR CONFINING FARM ANIMALS. INITIATIVE STATUTE. Requires that certain farm animals be allowed, for the majority of every day, to fully extend their limbs or wings, lie down, stand up and turn around. Limited exceptions

---

Dr. Minnie Ransom was so excited to vote for Barack Obama that she was the 4th person to submit her ballot before school so she could share with her students.

History Being Made

The New First Family Album

On Inauguration Day, Jan. 20, history will be made as 1600 Pennsylvania Ave. welcomes the 44th president, his wife and their children. USA WEEKEND introduces the Obamas.

▶ On the campaign trail, Obama takes time out for Sasha.

▲ Barack Obama in his Chicago kitchen in 2006, with Malia, then 8, and Sasha, then 5.

▶ The president-elect drops the kids off at school.

▲ Three generations: First lady Michelle Obama, Malia, now 10, *left*, and Sasha, now 7, and Michel granny" Marian Robinson, show support for their a 2007 Women for Obama festival in New Hamps

Cover photograph by Kwaku

▼ The happy family enjoys a Fourth of July parade in 2008.

▲ Michelle and Sasha listen as Obama speaks on the trail.

▼ Sasha and Michelle at a Fourth of July picnic last summer in Montana.

Vacationing in Hawaii, Obama's birth state

Obama plays soccer with Malia on her 10th birthday.

▲ Barack and Michelle Obama, married for 16 years, trade smiles.

Exclusive: Michelle Obama on what matters most now
TURN THE PAGE >>

Broderick Stephen Harvey (1957 –)

Steve Harvey was born on January 17, 1957
in Welch, West Virginia.
He is the son of a coal miner.
Steve was determined to be a successful career climber.
His first name is Broderick,
named after the actor Broderick Crawford, somewhat ironic.
The actor stared in the TV series *Highway Patrol*.
Seeking for a better life than that coal mining hellhole,
the Harvey family relocated to Cleveland, Ohio.
They lived on East 112th Street, a much better scenario.
Steve was surprised on his 50th birthday with the street
being named in his honor on his tv show.

He graduated from Glenville High School in 1974.
Shortly after high school, barely out the door,
he attended Kent State University
and West Virginia University.
He is a member of Omega Psi Phi fraternity.

Steve Harvey has been a mailman, an autoworker,
an insurance salesman, a carpet cleaner, and a boxer.
He first performed stand-up comedy on October 8, 1985,
at the Hilarities Comedy Club in Cleveland, Ohio,
with a burning desire to thrive.

In the late '80s, Steve was homeless for three years.
He would do whatever it took, and to the plan to adhere.
He slept in his 1976 Ford when the performances did not
provide a hotel, and he showered at gas stations

to keep going and not have things to worsen.
He also would shower in swimming pool showers.
He is a fashionable man and looking good,
he had to smell like a flower.

Rich and Becky Liss (a White couple) assisted Steve during
these times with a contract for carpet cleaning and credit
at a travel agency.
Then in 1997, Steve could prolong his work in stand-up comedy,
performing on the tour Kings of Comedy.
On National TV, when his staff surprised him for his birthday
with a satellite call from the Lisses,
Steve broke down. He could not hold his composure, no way!

The tour became the highest grossing comedy tour in history,
grossing $18 million its first year and $19 million its second.
Later it was put into a film, the act of comedy.
Spike Lee called it, *The Original Kings of Comedy*.
Steve Harvey has authored four books, including his bestseller,
Act Like a Lady, Think Like a Man, released in 2009.

In 2015, East 112th Street, was renamed Steve Harvey Way.
Honor and recognition to Steve Harvey, they would pay.

In 2017, Harvey founded Steve Harvey Global,
an entertainment theater company that houses his productions.
Company East 112 and various other undertakings of his decisions
were sufficient for his creations.
He and his wife, Marjorie are the founders of,
The Steve and Marjorie Harvey Foundation,
a nonprofit organization focused on youth education.

Steve's released book in 2009, *Act Like a Lady,*
Think Like a Man is about how men think about women
and relationships. The 2012 film, *Think Like a Man*,

was an ensemble romantic comedy depicting characters
taking advice on dating from the book. The hardcover
version spent 64 weeks on The New York Times best-seller
list, 23 of those weeks at number one.
Steve began hosting *Family Feud* in September 2010
that had seen improved ratings surpassed every
previous *Feud* host.

On August 2, 2012, Steve presented his final stand-up
act at the MGM Grand in Las Vegas, ending a 27-year career
as a stand-up comedian to fear.
The two-hour performance was broadcast live on Pay-Per-View.
He performed his last standup show, the *Kings of Comedy
Tour* in 2012.
He received Ebony Magazine's Man of the Year award on
May 13, 2013.
In 2013, Steve became the first double host nominated
for a *Daytime Emmy Award*, receiving nominations for both
Outstanding Talk Show Host and *Outstanding Game Show* Host.
He was also honored with a star on the *Hollywood Walk of Fame.*

The following year, Steve launched a new dating website
Called, *Delightful.*
In January 2016, Steve gave a motivational speech to audience
after the taping of an episode of *Family Feud.*
The theme of the speech was for people to embrace their skills.
He referred to embracing the gifts with jumping from a cliff
and relying on the parachute (those gifts) to help you.
The speech was the motivation for the book *Leap:
Take the Leap of Faith to Achieve Your Life of Abundance,*
published by Steve in 2016.

Steve is the co-creator of *Little Big Shots*, a series launched
in 2016 and executive produced by him.
The series features children
exhibiting talents and participating in dialogue with him.
Steve hosted the show until 2019.

He is a six-time *Daytime Emmy Award* winner, two-time *Marconi
Award* winner, and a 14-time *NAACP Image Award* winner in the
various categories.

Steve is businessman, comedian, actor, broadcaster,
author, game show host, and a television presenter.
Steve is a romantic. Married three times with an average
of two years between each divorce and marriage,
advising women and interactions through his book,
and unveiled a dating website hook-up.

Before the broadcast of the New Year's Eve special
from Times Square for Fox, in two days he was ordained.
He wanted it right and being ordained was essential.
He was ordained in the state of New York so he could
officiate an on-air wedding between Keven Undergaro
and Matia Menounos in 2017.
The special was Fox's most-watched New Year's
Eve broadcast.

Steve Harvey continues to perform various business ventures
with his family, different networks, and partnerships
with varied abilities.
He continues to be one of America's favorite television personalities.

John Wesley Carlos (1945 –)

John Wesley Carlos was born June 5,1945 in the Bronx.
He was raised in Harlem, New York.
His mother was born in Jamaica West Indies and grew up in Cuba.
His father was a World War I veteran and was from Camden,
South Carolina.
John was a talented athlete and exceptional student in high school.
He later studied at East Texas State University on a full track-and-field
scholarship.
He had excellent sportsmanship.
He assisted in the 100, 200-meter dash, and as a participant of the
4×400-meter relay to advantage ETSU to the 1967 Lone Star
Conference Championship.
After his first year, John enrolled at San Jose State University.
He would coach Lloyd (Bud) Winter as a trainer.
He would be a future National Track & Field Hall of Famer

In the 200 meters at the 1967 Pan American Games in Winnipeg,
Manitoba, Canada he was the gold medalist.
In the 60-yard dash and the 220-yard dash he set indoor world bests.
John had his greatest year in track and field in 1969,
leading San Jose State to its first NCAA championship with victories
in the 100, 220, and as a member of the 4×110-yard relay.
He was presented on the cover of Track and Field News in May 1969.

Initially all Black athletes were urged to boycott the Mexico City
Olympics of 1968.
The slow progress of the civil rights movement they were to protest.
When the boycott failed to gain support, the decision was
left to individual athletes to protest.

John and Tommie Smith, a fellow athlete took up the charge. After
    finishing first and third in the 200-meter Olympic final and
    Tommie
setting a world record, they decided that they would use the medal
ceremony to make a gesture on American bigotry.
The two removed their shoes and wore black socks to signify
black poverty.
They had each planned to wear black gloves to represent black power
and unity.
Tommie wore a black scarf and John wore beads lynchings they would
signify.

Their Black Power salute on the podium caused much
    political controversy.
John went on to tie the world record in the 100-yard dash and beat
the 200 meters world history.
Peter Norman, the silver medalist who was a white athlete
    from Australia,
participated with John and Tommie to protest racial inequality by
    wearing
an OPHR (The Olympic Project for Human Rights) badge in solidary.
The badge was created because of segregation in the United States,
elsewhere, and racism in sports.

In response to their actions, Tommie and John were ordered to be
suspended from the US team and banned from the Olympic Village.
This was supposed to send a "No Protesting" message.
When the US Olympic Committee refused, the entire US track
    team was
threatened to be banned.
This would make everyone understand their command.
The results were for the two athletes from the games elimination.
At the Berlin Olympics, against the Nazi salutes, there had not been
made any objections.

It was argued that at the time the Nazi salute, being a national salute, in a competition of nations it was acceptable.
The athletes' salute was not of a nation and therefore unacceptable.
After John's track career, he played in the Canadian Football League.
He retired due to injury.
He became involved with the United States Olympic Committee.
He helped to organize the 1984 Summer Olympics.

John Carlos is former track and field athlete and professional football player.
In the 200 meters at the 1968 Summer Olympics, he was the bronze-medal winner.
Of the Olympic Project for Human Rights (OPHR), John Carlos became a founding member.
A boycott of the 1968 Mexico City Olympic Games he originally advocated.
Without the support instead in the protest he participated.

In 1985, John became an in-school suspension supervisor.
He additionally became a counselor.
He was a track trainer as well at Palm Springs High School.
He was the USA Track & Field Hall of Fame inductee.
In 2003.
He is the creator, with sportswriter Dave Zirin, of *The John Carlos Story: The Sports Moment That Changed the World*, that was published in 2011.
In 2005, A statue exhibiting John and Tommie on the award stand was constructed by a political artist and donated to the campus of San Jose State University.
In 2006, he and Tommie Smith were pallbearer at Peter Norman's ceremony.
John Carlos delivered the eulogy at the service.
In 2007, John Carlos was honored at the Trumpet Awards in Las Vegas, Nevada.

In April 2008, John was a torchbearer for the Human Rights Torch running parallel to the 2008 Summer Olympics torch relay.
It focused attention on China's human rights record.
On July 16, 2008, John Carlos and Tommie Smith accepted the Arthur Ashe Award for Courage for their salute, at the 2008 ESPY Awards held at NOKIA Theatre L.A. LIVE in Los Angeles, California.
In July 2018, John Carlos attended the Socialism 2018 conference hosted by the International Socialist Organization.
In 2008 John was awarded from California State University.
a doctorate honorary.
In 2012, he was awarded honorary doctorates from Texas A&M University-
Commerce (formerly East Texas State University)
and San Jose State University.

> *"Today I am here for you. Why? Because I am you. We are here forty-three years later because there is a fight still to be won. This day is not for us but for our children to come."*
>
> —*by John Wesley Carlos*

Muhammad Ali (1942 – 2016)

Muhammad Ali was born in Kentucky on January 17, 1942
in Louisville.
He began training as an amateur boxer. At age of 12,
demonstrating boxing skills.
His father was a sign painter and his mother cleaned houses
when money was low to help pay the bills.
Muhammad Ali had one sibling, an older brother who also was a boxer.
Young Muhammad was taken to Baptist church every
Sunday by his mother.
At 18, he participated in the 1960 Summer Olympics
in the light heavyweight division.
Muhammad Ali won a gold medal was the decision.
He turned professional later that year.
In his prime, he defiantly was a boxer that was to fear.

Muhammad Ali was young, skilled, and very athletic.
His dancing and rhyming made most become loyal fanatics.
He had a unique talent of boxing.
Muhammad Ali made up rhymes that he repeated to fit the occasion.
He would irritate his opponent before and
during the match sometime with his end of bout prediction.

Muhammad Ali became a Muslim after 1961.
At an early age, he realized that freedom of Blacks still
needed to be won.

Ali registered for the draft in the United States military on his
18th birthday and was listed as 1-A in 1962.

Muhammad Ali won the world heavyweight championship from
    Sonny Liston
in a major upset on February 25, 1964, at age 22.
On March 6, 1964, he revealed that he no longer would be known
as *Cassius Clay* but as Muhammad Ali.
Muhammad Ali was serious about it extremely.
He was known to correct many even in the boxing ring.

In 1964, he was reclassified as Class 1-Y
Muhammad Ali failed the U.S. Armed Forces qualifying test
because his writing and spelling skills were not the best.
He did not meet specification due to his dyslexia.
He was quoted as saying, "I said I was the greatest, not the smartest!"
Muhammad Ali was always funny but honest.

By early 1966, the army reduced its standards to permit soldiers
above the 15th percentile.
Amazing the law if need be, was one retractile.

Ali was again categorized as 1-A. This category now required
that he was for the draft and induction into the U.S. Army
    now qualified.
To send him to Vietnam War was the intent,
but to his views they would not listen. They were inanimate.
This put him further at odds with the white institution.
Ali had made his views on the issue clear with public confessions.

When notified of this status, Ali declared that he would refuse to serve.
Muhammad Ali felt that taking the people's lives there, they did
    not deserve.
He felt that killing people in another country not his enemy
    was absurd.
He felt that the people there were not his suppressors.
Muhammad Ali publicly considered himself a conscientious objector.
Ali provoked the white establishment in 1966 by refusing the draft

into the U.S. military who were not going to fight his adversary.
An officer warned him that he was committing a felony
punishable by five years in prison and a fine of $10,000.
Muhammad Ali cited his religious beliefs and ethical opposition to
    the Vietnam War.
He was arrested, his boxing licenses were suspended, and denied
systematically.

Muhammad Ali was found guilty of draft evasion.
The nation and world began to awaken.
He faced 5 years in prison and was stripped of his boxing titles.
Other boxing commissions followed suit.
Things and lives had been taken from activist fighting for the cause,
but no one had put their all on the line and at the peak of their career
for any movement had anyone taken this path.

Ali remained unable to acquire a license to box in any state.
His actions started to open everyone's eyes on hate.
Muhammad Ali stayed out of custody as he appealed the verdict
of the Supreme Court.
Would he be able to continue his career in sports?

On June 4, 1967, in a first for sports professionals,
a group of high-profile Black American athletes met
at the Negro Industrial Economic Union in Cleveland.
They wanted to see what they could do for the icon.
The meeting was organized by Jim Brown of his peers.
It gave Ali the chance to express in detail his ideas.
They would question Ali about the seriousness of his convictions.
To support him or not, they would be coming to a decision,
and to hear his views would give them all a rare opportunity.
Afterwards, they supported Ali whole-heartly.

At the trial on June 20, 1967, the jury found Ali guilty
after only 21 minutes of deliberation.
A Court of Appeals upheld the conviction.
The case was reviewed by the U.S. Supreme Court in 1971.
His conviction was overturned by unanimous 8–0 in 1971.
Justice Thurgood Marshall disqualified himself.
He had been the U.S. Legal Representative at the time
of Ali's conviction.
To limit problems, surround this, he made the wise decision.
The appeal board gave no reason for the denial of a conscientious
objector exemption.
The conscientious objector conviction had to be reversed
for Ali's conviction.
It was impossible to determine which of the three basic tests
offered in the Justice Department's brief the appeal board relied
on for the conscientious objector status.
Initially when he refused induction, he received many death threats.
In the country he became the man most despised.
His whole world had capsized.

People who supported Ali during this time were also threatened.
Ali's example eventually began to inspire others.
Many Black Americans, and civil rights celebrities came to believe
that Ali had an energizing effect on the freedom movement.
He was putting everything on the line for what he believed
    was right.
His all he voluntarily sacrificed.
He demonstrated a different kind of leadership.
Later many learned that he was right.
What he received in return was cruel treatments.

In 1970, Ali was honored with the annual Martin Luther King Award
by civil rights leader Ralph Abernathy, who called him "a living
example
of soul power" of which Blacks were working toward.
The March on Washington with two fists, Coretta Scott King
added that Ali was "a champion of justice, peace, and unity."
He was standing up for what he believed more actively.
His trainer said that he was robbed of his best years, his prime years.
He did what he felt was right, not for cheers.

He found a five-acre site on a Pennsylvania country road in the village
of Deer Lake.
On this site, Ali carved out what was to become his training camp,
where he trained for all his fights from 1972 to the end of his career
in 1981.

In 1976, an inventor and businessman partnered with Ali to promote
The International Committee to Reunite the Beatles.
They asked fans worldwide to contribute a dollar each.
Ali said the idea was not to use the proceeds for profit, but to establish
an international agency to help poor children.
It would be money to help people all over the world.
He said that he loved music and trained while listening to their music.
He said that a reunion would make a lot of people happy.
The reunion never happened due to skeptics.

He had not fought for nearly four years and lost a period of peak performance as an athlete.

Ali›s actions as a conscientious objector to the Vietnam War made him an icon for the generation opposing the social norm of the day.

He was a very high-profile figure of racial pride for Blacks during the civil rights movement and throughout his career.

He was involved in several historic boxing matches.

Ali blossomed in the spotlight of the media at a time when many fighters let their managers do the talking.

He was often confrontational and unusual with his rhyming, jokes, much loved humor.

He loved to trash-talk his opponents and the news reporters.

He often would adapt rhymes and lecture his opponents.

He would proclaim that he was the "greatest" and would live up to be just that.

He would also say that he was, "Pretty"! He had a method of keeping the opponent from hitting him in his face during matches. Therefore after a fight you would not see his face bruised because they could not catch him to land punches in this face.

One of his favorite saying was, "Float like a butterfly. Sting like a bee." They could not catch Muhammad Ali.

He has been ranked the greatest heavyweight boxer of all time.

He was ranked the greatest sportsman of the 20th century by *Sports Illustrated* and the Sports Personality of the Century by the BBC.

Ali attained success as a spoken word artist.
He received two Grammy nominations.
Ali was an American professional boxer, activist, entertainer, poet, and philanthropist.
His Nickname was "The Greatest". He is widely regarded as one of the most
significant and celebrated sporting figures of the 20ᵗʰ century.
He is frequently ranked as the best heavyweight boxer
and greatest athlete of the century. He has been featured as an actor and writer.
He also has released two autobiographies.

Ali retired from boxing in 1981 and focused on religion, philanthropy and activism.

In 1984, he made public his diagnosis of Parkinson's syndrome.
Even though he and his specialist physicians disputed, many believed his diagnosis was due to boxing-related injuries.
He remained an active public figure globally,
but in his later years made fewer public appearances as his condition worsened.

Ali was married four times and had seven daughters and two sons.
His first wife was said to be his true love.
He met her through a friend and was married about one month afterwards.
She would not convert to the Muslim lifestyle which caused friction between them. They did not have children.
His second wife and her family had converted to the Nation of Islam.
She later changed her name to a Muslim name and had 4 children.
At age 32 in 1974, Ali began an extramarital relationship with
a 16-year-old with whom he fathered another daughter.

He married her in an Islamic ceremony that was not legally recognized.
They all lived on his training camp with his family.
January 1985, Ali was sued for unpaid palimony.
The case was settled when Ali agreed to set up a $200,000 trust fund for
the illegitimate child.
He had another daughter from another extramarital relationship.
By the summer of 1977, his second marriage ended due to Ali's repeated infidelity.
He married an actress and model who at the time of their marriage
    had a
daughter and she was pregnant with their second child.
By 1986, they were divorced due to Ali's continuous infidelity.
On November 19, 1986, Ali married again to a lady he had first met when she was 6 years old.
In 1982, she became Ali's primary caregiver and in return,
he paid for her to attend graduate school at U.C.L.A.
Together they adopted a son when he was five months old.
In 1992, she incorporated Greatest of All Time, Inc. (G.O.A.T. Inc)
to consolidate and license his intellectual properties for commercial purposes.
She served as the vice president and treasurer until the sale of the company in 2006.

Since his death, there have been other claims of him being their father as well.

Ali's had one daughter that was a professional boxer from 1999 until 2007, despite her father's previous opposition to women boxing.
One daughter is the wife of a middleweight boxer.

She stated that his love for people was extraordinary.

She said she would get home from school to find homeless families sleeping in their guest room.

He would see them on the street, pile them into his Rolls-Royce and take them home.

He would buy them clothes, take them to hotels, and pay the bills for months in advance. He wanted people to be happy.

After the conversion to Muslim, Ali's Muslim family became his family and Elijah Muhammad became his father.

There is an irony to the fact that while the Nation branded white people as
devils, Ali had more white colleagues than most Black American people did
at that time in America.

He continued to have them throughout his career.

He later renounced the Nation and supporting racial integration like his
former mentor Malcolm X.

He was cared for by his family until his death on June 3, 2016.

> *"My enemy is the white people, not Viet Cong or Chinese or Japanese. You my opposer when I want freedom. You my opposer when I want justice. You my opposer when I want equality. You won't even stand up for me in America for my religious beliefs—and you want me to go somewhere and fight, but you won't even stand up for me here at home?"*

> *"We are not to be the aggressor, but we will defend ourselves if attacked." "Man, I ain't got no quarrel with them Viet Cong." "Why should they ask me to put on a uniform and go ten thousand miles from home and drop bombs and bullets on brown people in Vietnam while so-called Negro people in Louisville are treated like dogs and denied simple human rights?"*

"If they say stand and salute the flag, I do that out of respect, because I'm in the country". "If America was in trouble and real war came, I'd be on the front line if we had been attacked. But I could see that (The Vietnam War) wasn't right". "Black men would go over there and fight, but when they came home, they couldn't even be served a hamburger."

"I am America. I am the part you won't recognize. But get used to me. Black, confident, cocky; my name, not yours; my religion, not yours; my goals, my own; get used to me."

"God created all people, no matter what their religion". "If you're against someone because he's a Muslim that's wrong. If you're against someone because he's a Christian or a Jew, that's wrong"

—by Muhammad Ali

Muhammad Ali
https://www.loc.gov/item/2020729681/

https://www.loc.gov/item/2015649460/
Muhammad Ali and Rosa Parks during the Brotherhood
Crusade tribute to Parks and Muhammad Ali, Los Angeles,
California, 1994

Emmett Till (1941 – 1955)

Emmett was born on July 25, 1941, in Chicago, IL.
Emmett was the only child of Louis and Mamie Till.
He grew up on Chicago's South Side.
He was barely 14 years old when he died.
He lived in a thriving, middle-class Black neighborhood.
The neighborhood was a haven for Black-owned businesses.
The variety and success for some cities in comparison,
the city surpasses.
The streets he played on as a child were lined
with Black-owned successful businesses.

Emmett was also known for being a practical joker
and a sharp dresser.
His mother took care of him. He was not a gangster.
The only photographs of him always showed him in a dress
shirt and tie, and occasionally wearing a pork pie hat.
By the time he turned 14, Emmett had grown husky.
For his size and style of dress, he could easily pass for an actor.

Emmett was responsible at a young age.
His mother often worked 10 hours a day.
He told his mom if she worked and made the money,
he would do everything else.
He took over all the household chores and still had time to play.

He was a happy-go-lucky child and playful.
He had a likable smile and loved to make people laugh.
He was about 5 feet, 4 inches and weighed about 150 pounds.
Emmett was raised by his mother and grandmother.

The family had migrated to Chicago, from Mississippi
when his mother was a child.
They lived in a cozy two-flat brick home in a middle-class
neighborhood on the city's South Side.

Emmett's mother was an exceptional woman.
The social restrictions of discrimination she was resisting.
She faced it as a Black American woman growing up
in the 1930s and 1920s.
Her way of fighting back was, she excelled both
scholastically and professionally.
She was one of the fourth Black student to graduate only
From Chicago's suburban Argo Community High School
that was white predominantly.

She was the first Black student to make the school's Honor Roll.
While raising Emmett as a single mother, she worked long hours
to meet her career goals.
She worked for the Air Force as a clerk in charge of confidential files
of which every day, there were piles.

Emmett never knew his father.
He was a private in the United States Army during World War II.
Emmett was born in 1941. His parents his parents separated in 1942.
Three years later, his mother received word from the Army his father
had been executed for "willful misconduct" while serving in Italy.
Emmett was just shy of his fourth birthday in 1945.
His father was only 23.
He had been executed by hanging after being found of rape, guilty
and murder while stationed in Italy.
Two years later, at age 6, Emmett developed polio,
which apparently left him with a speech obstacle.

Earlier that summer, his great-uncle, a sharecropper in the
Mississippi Delta came to Chicago telling tales remarkable.
about life in the country and Emmett was intrigued.
His mother allowing him to go to visit consented
instead of traveling with her to Nebraska for summer break
a visit to his uncle's place he would take.
She give Emmett a dire warning about racial friction in the South.
She knew it was extremely dangerous time for Black people
and warned her only son to carefully watch his words from his mouth.
To also watch his manners around white people.
Racial tensions were running hot in 1955,
She was giving him tips to survive.
A year after the U.S. Supreme Court ended racial
segregation in public facilities.
While visiting his uncle, on August 24, he was with his cousins
and some friends at a country store.
He bought some candy and was accused of assaulting
the White store owner's wife.

One version of the events was said that Emmett whistled
suggestively either as a joke or a dare with his friends,
but other accounts disputed this claim, saying Emmett
whistled outside the store but never toward a woman.
When some of the townspeople in the area at the time warned
the boys to flee, the boys left immediately.
Word spread like wildfire about the incident apparently,
fueled by the false perception that a Black person had possibly
attacked a white woman.

The woman's husband learned what occurred.
He was furious that his wife had not told him what he had heard.
He took it upon himself to investigate and in his rage.
turned from grocer to vigilante.
It was said that he searched the town the same night
with his half-brother.

It did not take him long to learn who Emmett Till
was and where he was staying.
They found Emmett's uncle's house about 3 o'clock in the morning,
They broke inside and snatched child from his bed who was sleeping.
They made Emmett carry a 75-pound cotton gin fan to the bank
of the Tallahatchie River and ordered him to take off his clothes.
The two men then beat him nearly to death, gouged out his eye,
shot him in the head, and then threw his body, tied to the cotton
gin fan with barbed wire around his neck, into the river.
Three days later, he was found.

He was unrecognizable to his uncle except by an initialed ring.
Authorities wanted to bury the body quickly, but Emmett's mother,
requested her only son's body to be sent back to Chicago.
The violent senseless murders of her child simply because of the color
of his skin, she wanted the world to know.
His mother wanted the world to see the savage brutality that her
son was forced to endure.
Bodies in that shape would have been a closed casket service for sure.
Those who carried out the premeditated hate crimes like the one
of Emmett had never been held responsible.
Whatever they did to Blacks was not accountable.
If taken to court, the law would not find their acts unlawful.

Less than two weeks after Emmett's body was buried,
the Bryant brothers went on trial in a segregated courthouse
in Mississippi but they were not worried.
There were few witnesses besides Emmett's uncle,
who positively identified the defendants as Emmett's killers.
On September 23, the all-white jury deliberated for less than an hour
before issued a verdict of "not guilty."
They said that the state had failed to prove the identity of the body.

62 years later, in 2017, Carolyn Bryant recanted her testimony,
admitting that Emmett had never touched, threatened, or
harassed her.

Emmett lived only one month past his 14th birthday.
His cold-blooded murder was predetermined by the color of his skin
and the greater forces of systemic racism they convey.
Systemic racism including lynchings had already been deeply woven.
in the fabric of the nation many years before his birth even.

By the time Emmett's short life began in 1941,
lynchings of Black people had become a dirty, concealed,
and customary feature of Black American's lives especially
throughout the South in the decades after the Civil War.

During the eras of Reconstruction, Jim Crow and civil rights,
bands of white vigilantes usually led by the Ku Klux Klan
were notorious for carrying out lynchings, bombings,
and assassinations on Black people with immunity,
and freedom with no legal consequences.

Nearly all the slayings remain cold cases until today.
Historians say that lynchings, bombings, torture, and brutality
such as that of Emmett Till were designed
to instill terror in the Black community and set vicious examples
that would uphold the idea of white supremacy.

During the lynching era, it was not uncommon for the deaths
of Black men to be ruled as suicides to cover up murders by white
mobs and police officers, according to The Washington Post.
Mississippi law enforcement was notorious for turning a blind eye
to the racially motivated crimes.

At the time of Emmett's murder, Black people still did not have the
right to vote.
Memories of the pervasive massacres are still an open wound
for Black communities.
They view modern-day police shootings as an extension
of the brutal era increasingly.
Emmette's death was a crucial piece of the civil rights struggle
and shined a spotlight on the of the Jim Crow South brutality.
His killing led to outward greater social change ultimately.

However, the hatred remained in the hearts and minds of some
which continued to bring about other forms of racism to come.
The videotaped death of George Floyd on Memorial Day,
May 25, 2020, as a Minneapolis police officer held him down
with a knee on his neck for nearly eight minutes sparked
protests around the world and reminded Black Americans
that the struggle over race is far from over.
As many saw it, it was a modern-day lynching.

Floyd lying powerlessly on the ground, pleading for his life,
complying, did not bring about a threat, clearly demonstrated
the cop's power over a Black man's life, a modern-day lynching!
Since Floyd's death, polls have revealed a dramatic shift
in how Americans view police violence, with people now viewing
the plight of Blacks differently. Now listening. Now hearing. Now
acknowledging. Now understand.

Congressman John Lewis (1940 – 2020)

John Robert Lewis was born February 21,1940 outside of Troy,
Alabama.
He was the son of sharecroppers.
He grew up on his family's farm.
In Pike County, Alabama he also attended public schools that were
segregated.
John Lewis developed at an early age, as he soon demonstrated.
He had a strong steadfast pull in his heart to the commitment
of the Civil Rights Movement.
His inspiration came from Dr. Martin Luther King, Jr., Rosa Parks,
and the Montgomery Bus Boycott of 1955-1956.
He was loving, honest, and kind.
Most of all he cared about mankind.
He was an excellent college scholar.
In 1959 in Nashville, Tennessee he organized sit-ins at lunch counters.

John earned from American Baptist Theological Seminary
a Bachelor of Divinity degree.
He also earned a bachelor's degree in religion and
Philosophy from Fisk University.

In 1960 he helped establish the Student Nonviolent Coordinating
Committee (SNCC).
Soon boosting him to national prominence was his true displayed
for human Rights, his unwavering leadership, activism, and bravery.
He became a Freedom Rider in 1961 traveling through the South
    with
white activists on interstate buses to protest segregation.
During the height of the Civil Rights Movement, from 1963 to

1966 of the Student Nonviolent Coordinating Committee (SNCC), he helped to form he was the Chairman.

SNCC was largely responsible for the sit-ins of students in the struggle for civil rights movement.

He was the youngest of the Civil Rights Movement's "Big Six," Leaders, SNCC (1963-1966) chairman.

At 23, he gave one of the keynote speeches at the 1963 March on Washington.

He planned and coordinated SNCC's in Freedom Summer of 1964 participation.

Black and White students went to the South to participate in movement actions.

On March 7, 1965, John and SCLC's Hosea Williams led the voting rights
march Selma to Montgomery.

After local authorities fractured John's skull, that day became known as "Bloody Sunday".

They also beat other marchers as they crossed the Edmond Pettus Bridge.

Following a televised petition by John, President Lyndon Johnson implored that the Voting Rights Act by Congress be passed.

Changing the laws of the past.

After departing SNCC in 1966, he was appointed by President Jimmy Carter to lead the Voter Education Project.

Later on, he directed the federal volunteer agency ACTION (1977 – 1980).

John Lewis was to lead more than 250,000 volunteers of ACTION.

John Lewis's first electoral success came in 1981.

The Atlanta City Council he had won.

While serving on the Atlanta City Council, John was an advocate for ethics in government and neighborhood preservation.

He was winning everyone's admiration.

He resigned from the Council in 1986 to run for Congress.

He was elected to Congress in November 1986.
Congressman John Lewis represents Georgia's Fifth
Congressional District.
In 1996, John Lewis was unopposed in his bid for a sixth term
and served up to his ninth term in office.

John Lewis dedicated his life to the non-violent struggle for social
change since his days in Tennessee as a student in seminary.
John displayed a sense of ethics and morality that won him the
admiration of many.

From colleges and universities throughout the United States
He was awarded numerous honorary degrees.
John Lewis was the recipient of numerous awards, including the
prestigious Martin Luther King, Jr. Non-Violent Peace Prize and the
NAACP Spingarn Medal.
John Lewis was the recipient of the John F. Kennedy "Profile in Courage
Award" for lifetime achievement and the National Education Association
Martin Luther King Jr. Memorial Award.
He was described as "One of the most courageous persons the Civil
Rights
Movement ever produced".
John Lewis dedicated his life to protecting human rights and securing
personal dignity.
Despite his youth, John Lewis became a recognized leader in the Civil
Rights Movement.

In the 108th Congress, Congressman John Lewis was a member
of the influential House Budget Committee and House Ways and
Means Committee.
He served on the Subcommittee on Health.
Congressman Lewis served as Senior Chief Deputy Democratic Whip.
He sat in a direct line of succession to the number two Democratic
leadership position in the House.

Congressman Lewis served on the Democratic Steering Committee.
He was a member of the Congressional Black Caucus and the
Congressional Committee to Support Writers and Journalists.
He served as Co-Chair of the Faith and Politics Institute.
In 1990, the National Journal named Congressman John Lewis as one of
eleven "rising stars in Congress."
The Journal stated, "Few House Members…have had such momentous
experiences before coming to Washington that other Members of
Congress wants to hear about them. John R. Lewis, D-GA., has that
cachet and he has made it a plus in his House service."
In 1998, Congressional Quarterly named Congressman John Lewis
a Liberal Stalwart in its edition "50 ways to do the job of Congress."

Congressman John Lewis had been summarized in numerous national
Publications, network television, radio broadcasts, as well as
a profile in a Time Magazine (Dec. 29, 1975) article called, "Saints
Among Us", and profiles in The New Yorker (Oct. 4, 1993).
He was also in Parade Magazine (Feb. 4, 1996), and The New Republic
(July 1, 1996).
Congressman John Lewis, with writer Michael D'Orso, authored
Walking
With The Wind: A Memoir of the Movement (June,1998). The
book is first-
hand account of this nation's civil rights movement.
Congressman John Robert Lewis was an American statesman and
civil rights activist who served in the United States House of
Representatives for Georgia's 5th congressional district from 1987
until his death July 17,2020, in Atlanta, GA.

Congressman John Lewis lived to build what he called, *"The Beloved Community"*

"get into good trouble, necessary trouble"; "Find a way to get in the way".

"When you see something that is not right, not fair, not just, you have to speak up…"

"The vote is the most powerful nonviolent tool we have…"

"Rioting is not a movement."

"Every generation leaves behind a legacy…"

"Never give up. Never give in. Never become hostile…Hate is too big a burden to bear."

—by John Lewis

Congressman John Lewis
https://tile.loc.gov/storage-services/service/pnp/
ppmsca/65400/65496v.jpg

Dr. Martin Luther King Jr. (1929 – 1968)

Dr. King was born on January 15, 1929, in Atlanta, Georgia.
The name on his initial birth documentation was Michael King
which was a mistake, not an uncommon thing.
He was expected to be named after his father who was
Martin Luther King.
He had an older sister and a younger brother.
He attended Booker T. Washington High School.
He was an excellent scholar with all the right tools.
Young Martin, the intelligent person that he was skipped
9th and 12th grades in high school, very well equipped.
He started his college education at Morehouse College.
at the young age of fifteen.

After getting his degree from Morehouse in sociology,
Martin received a divinity degree from Crozer Seminary.
Then he received his doctor's degree in theology from Boston University.
Martin's dad was a preacher inspiring Martin to pursue the ministry.
He became a minister at the age of 18.

He married Coretta Scott at the age of 24.
They had children four.
The author has had the pleasure of meeting his son,
Martin Luther King III on two occasions.

Dr. King led many marches and protests for equal justice for all people.
He was put in jail many times and on many other occasions,
his life was threatened.
That did not stop him from doing what he felt was right and fighting.

Dr. Martin Luther King, Jr. led the Montgomery Bus Boycott that started
when Rosa Parks refused to give up her seat on a bus to a white male.
It was almost 4 months after the brutal killing of Emmett Till.
She was arrested and spent the night in jail.
As a result, Martin helped to organize a boycott of the public
transportation system in Montgomery.
The boycott lasted for over a year. It was very tense times.
Martin was arrested and his house was bombed.
Black people did not ride the buses for over a year.
Black people stuck together, not riding the bus, making it very clear.
They carpooled or walked in all kinds of weather
on tired and sometimes feet so achy.
They refused to ride the buses running mostly empty.
In the end, however, Dr. King prevailed and the segregation on the
Montgomery buses came to an end.

1963, Dr. Martin Luther King, Jr. helped to organize the famous
"March on Washington".
Over 250,000 people attended this march to show the importance
of civil rights legislation affliction.
Some of the issues the march hoped to accomplish included an end
to public schools' segregation,
get laws passed that would prevent discrimination in employment, and
from police abuse, protection.

It was at this march where Dr. King gave his "I Have a Dream" speech.
This speech has become one of the most famous speeches in history.
The March on Washington was a great success.
Humankind was supposed to move forward, not regress.
The Civil Rights Act was passed a year later in 1964.
It was now illegal to discriminate against anyone anymore.

Dr. King was the youngest person to be awarded the Nobel Peace Prize in 1964.
Currently, Dr. Martin Luther King, Jr. Day is a national holiday.
At the Atlanta premier of the movie, *Gone with the Wind*, Dr. King sang with his church choir.

Sadly, his life was cut short on April 4, 1968, in Memphis, TN.
Dr. Martin Luther King, Jr. was assassinated
while standing on his hotel's balcony.
He was shot at the age of 39 years old by James Earl Ray.
He was assassinated while he was leading a protest to fight
against poverty.
Although he was taken from us, he will never be forgotten
for his vision for all mankind, his brave and unselfish impeccable character, his inspiring words and deeds,
helped millions of people of all races and creeds.
Dr. Martin Luther King, Jr. was a civil rights activist in the 1960s and 1950s.
He led non-violent protests for people's rights fights
for all people including, Blacks and Whites.
He hoped that America and the world could form a society
where race would not impact a person's civil rights.
He is still considered one of the great speakers of modern times, and his speeches still inspire all kind.

There are over 730 streets in the United States named
after Dr. Martin Luther King, Jr.
One of his main influences was Mohandas Gandhi who taught people to protest in a non-violent manner.
He was awarded the Congressional Gold Medal and the Presidential Medal of Freedom.
He was educated, and full of wisdom.
He is often referred to by his initials MLK.

There are many people that this author admires that did brave
and unselfish things to help others even though it would put their
lives and families in danger.
One of the people of our time is Dr. Martin Luther King Jr.
He was an educated, loyal, devoted family man, an inspirational
and a fabulous speaker.

He was religious and God was his armor and anchor.
He was respected in his community, devoted his life to
whatever he could do unselfishly to help everyone to receive equality
in an unequal society, and in a non-violent manner.
Quotes by Dr. Martin Luther King Jr.

> *"We must use time creatively, in the knowledge that the time is
> always ripe to do right."*
>
> *"A lie cannot live."*
>
> *"It is not enough to say we must not wage war. It is necessary
> to love peace and sacrifice for it".*
>
> *"Be a bush if you can't be a tree. If you can't be a highway, just
> be a trail. If you can't be a sun, be a star. For it isn't by size that
> you win or fail. Be the best of whatever you are."*
>
> *"A riot is the language of the unheard."*
>
> *"We must learn to live together as brothers or perish together
> as fools."*
>
> *"Mankind must put and end to war or war will put an end to
> mankind."*
>
> *—by Dr. Martin Luther King Jr.*

Dr. Martin Luther King Jr.
https://www.loc.gov/pictures/resource/yan.1a38887/

Sharonda (Dr. Minnie Ransom's daughter/a youth Usher) with **Martin Luther King III,** *and their pastor on one of his visits to their church in Union City, CA.*

Dr. Minnie Ransom *and* **Martin Luther King III** *on one of his visits to her church in Union City, CA.*

Malcolm X (1925 – 1965)

Malcolm Little was born on May 19, 1925, in Omaha, Nebraska.
His father, Earl Little, was a leader in a Black group called the UNIA.
His family moved around often while he was a child, but he spent
much of his childhood in East Lansing, Michigan.
The family was harassed by the Ku Klux Klan and white
supremacists often.
He had a traumatic childhood plagued by racism.

They once even had their house burnt down.
When Malcolm was six, his father was found dead on the tracks
of the local streetcar.
The police said the death was an accident which was too bizarre.
Many believed his dad was murdered.
Everyone knew the killers would not be discovered.
Malcolm's mother was left on her own to raise seven children.
To make matters worse, this occurred during the Great Depression.
Although his mom worked relentlessly and constantly,
Malcolm and his family were always hungry.

For several years, after the death of her husband his mother suffered
from emotional breakdown complications.
She was committed to a mental institution.
Into various foster homes and orphanages, they split up her children.

When Malcolm went to live with a foster family, he was 13 years of age.
He dropped out of school altogether at 15 years of age.
He faced racial discrimination from teachers in the eighth grade.
He was an excellent student and later in life regretted
not completing his education, not for a degree, but for the knowledge.

As a young black man Malcolm felt he had no real opportunities
despite how hard he worked in the 1940s.
He worked odd jobs but felt he would never thrive.
He could not make it working any job no matter the drive.
To make ends meet, he eventually turned to crime.
In 1945 he was caught with stolen goods and sent to prison to do time.

While in prison, Malcolm's brother sent him a letter about a new religion.
He had joined this new religion called the Nation of Islam.
The Nation of Islam believed that Islam was the true religion
of black people.
That made sense to Malcolm. He decided to join the Nation of Islam.
He also changed his last name to "X." He said the "X" represented
his real African name from him the white people had taken.

After getting out of prison, for the Nation of Islam, Malcolm
became a minister.
He worked at several temples around the country and of Temple Number
7 in Harlem he became the leader.
Malcolm was a born leader and a powerful speaker.
He was an impressive man.
He was an activist for the rights of humans.
He became a popular figure during the civil rights revolution.
He is best known for his time spent as a vocal spokesman
for the Nation of Islam.

Betty Sanders, who became Betty X, in 1958 married Malcolm.
They had together six daughters.
The girls did not have any brothers.
He became close friends with boxing champ Muhammad Ali.
Wherever Malcolm X went the Nation of Islam grew rapidly.
Muhammad Ali was also a member at the time of the Nation of Islam.
It was not long before Malcolm X was the second most influential
member of the Nation of Islam after their leader, Elijah Muhammad.

When the Black Civil Rights Movement began to gain momentum
in the 1960s, Malcolm was skeptical.
The peaceful protests of Dr. Martin Luther King, Jr. did not meet his
approval.
Malcolm did not want a nation where blacks and whites were integrated.
Racial pride, self-defense, and other ideas he articulated.
The Black Power movement emerging in the 1960s and '70s used those
same ideological mainstays.
He also wanted a separate nation just for black people.

As Malcolm's fame grew, other leaders of the Nation of Islam
became envious.
Malcolm also had some concerns about the behavior of Elijah
    Muhammad
as their mentor.
After teaching all his rules to follow of sternness and strictness
of the nation. He was not adhering to any of them as a leader.

Malcolm found out that the nation was built on too many lies to ignore.
Elijah had been having extramarital affairs that also resulted in children.
Malcolm had remained celibate until his marriage and then no
outside affairs.
Elijah pleaded for Malcolm to help him cover up the affairs and children
in despair.
Malcolm refused. He was deeply hurt by the deception.
He also felt guilty about all the people he had led to join the nation
that he now knew was a fraud and dysfunction.

When President John F. Kennedy
was assassinated, Malcolm was told by Elijah Muhammad not to discuss
the subject in public.
Elijah was worried about his unethical behavior reaching the public
    so toxic.
Malcolm spoke out anyway.

This created bad publicity for the Nation of Islam and Malcolm
   was ordered
to remain silent for 90 days.

He left the Nation of Islam. but he was still a Muslim.
He made a pilgrimage to Mecca where he had a change of heart over
the beliefs of the Nation of Islam.
Upon his return he began to work with other civil rights leaders like Dr.
Martin Luther King, Jr. on ways to peacefully achieve equal rights.
He finally saw Dr. King's dream and ultimate path for our plight.

Malcolm had made many enemies within the Nation of Islam.
Many leaders spoke out against him.
They felt that he did not deserve another breath.

On February 14, 1965, his house was burned down. A few days later
on February 21st as Malcolm began a speech in New York City,
he was gunned down by three members of the Nation of Islam
shooting him 15 times killing him at the age of 39 years old.

His autobiography was written by Alex Haley based on his interview
of Malcolm X.
Alex took up writing to avoid boredom while he served in the
U.S. Coast Guard.
Alex Haley later also wrote Roots connecting Black people to their
   ancestors
in Africa with positive characteristics of which we are survivors.
Both were created into movies.
Later both were also recognized as classics of African
   American literature.

> *"Education is the passport to the future, for tomorrow belongs
> to those who prepare for it today."*

> *"You can't separate peace from freedom because no one can be
> at peace unless he has his freedom."*

"We didn't land on Plymouth Rock, my brothers and sisters— Plymouth Rock landed on us."

"I believe in the brotherhood of man, all men, but I don't believe in brotherhood with anybody who doesn't want brotherhood with me. I believe in treating people right, but I'm not going to waste my time trying to treat somebody right who doesn't know how to return the treatment."

—by Malcolm X

Malcolm X
https://tile.loc.gov/storage-services/service/pnp/
vrg/12900/12978v.jpg

Jackie Robinson (1919 – 1972)

Jack Roosevelt Robinson was born January 31, 1919 in Cairo, Georgia.
His middle name was Roosevelt in respect of President
    Theodore Roosevelt.
He was the son of sharecroppers.
His grandparents were raised up as slaves in Georgia.
Jackie's father left the family just after he was born.
Jackie never saw him again.
He was the youngest of five children.
His mother was a strong woman.
She raised him and his three brothers and one sister.
She relocated to Pasadena about a year after.

In Pasadena, she worked as a maid cleaning the floor.
He attended public schools. The family was poor.
At Muir Technical High School, he demonstrated abilities in sports.
He excelled in basketball, football, track, and baseball.
He was excellent in all sorts.

However, without money or a scholarship and facing discrimination
Jackie could not display or be rewarded for his competencies.
All through high school Jackie had to deal with racism.
He attended a junior college excelling in football and baseball.
Most of his teammates were white and, while people would cheer
him on the field, they made it very clear.
Off the field he was treated as a second-class citizen.

Jackie grew up watching his older brothers excel in sports.
Jackie also loved to play sports.
In high school he ran track like his older brother. He also exhorts

to play other sports like football, baseball, tennis, and basketball.
He was the quarterback of the football team and the star baseball
player on the team.
His brother Mack became a track star who won a silver medal
in the 200-meter dash on the 1936 Olympics team.

After two years in junior college, he attended the University of
     California
at Los Angeles playing basketball, baseball, and football. He excelled
in all three.
He was the first athlete at UCLA to earn varsity letters in all
     four sports.
He also won the NCAA Championship in the long jump.
On his road to an education, he had also just hit another bump.
In 1941, he was forced to leave college due to financial problems.
With all that talent, there was no one to assist. He just
became another victim.

He played professional football until he was drafted into the Army
to serve in World War II.
Jackie met the legendary boxing champion Joe Lewis at basic
     training
and they became friends there too.

Joe helped Jackie get accepted into officer training school.
He was sent to Fort Hood, Texas to unite with the 761st Tank
     Battalion
once he completed the training of officer.
This battalion was made up of only Black soldiers
because they were not allowed to perform together with White soldiers.
Jackie got into trouble one day while riding a bus for
the army when he refused to move to the back.
He almost got booted out of the army,
but left with an honorable discharge in 1944.

Following the war, he coached briefly at Sam Houston College
   in Texas.
Later he signed on with a professional Black baseball team, the Kansas
City Monarchs.
During a championship game he was recognized for his abilities
   by Branch
Rickey, the president of the Brooklyn Dodgers.
He needed somebody who could take all the insults and not fight back.
Jackie signed with the Dodgers on October 23, 1945.
He would be the first Black to play on the all-White team.

In 1946 Jackie married and they had three children.
His family would be his anchor and support him.

He played on the Dodgers farm team, the Montreal Royals.
His first game on April 18, 1946, at his second at-bat he hit a
three-run home run.
He had made three more hits scoring four times and stole two bases
when it was all said and done.
By completion of the series, all could see that he had played a vital part
in the Little World Series.
Taking his team to victory was witnessed by even the bullies.

He had to deal with constant racism. Jackie held his anger inside
and played hard.
Sometimes the other team would not show up for the game
because of Jackie but he did not let down his guard.
People would yell at him, threaten him, or throw things at him.
He led the league and won the league's MVP award.
Breaking the Color Barrier at the start of the 1947 baseball season,
Jackie was called up to join the Brooklyn Dodgers. On April 15, 1947.
He became the first Black to play baseball in the major leagues.
He had moved up to first baseman by 1947.
He suffered harassment, black cats thrown on the field, and many

other humiliations.
Jackie faced all sorts of racial abuse from other baseball players
and from the fans.
His sportsmanship and composure throughout it all he maintained.
He even received death threats.
However, Jackie showed the courage to not fight back.
Focusing on playing baseball he lived up to his promise to
    Branch Rickey.
The Dodgers won the pennant and Rookie of the Year was Jackie.

Over the next ten years, Jackie Robinson was one of the best baseball
players in the major leagues.
He proved that he was worthy of his history making role.
Branch Rickey and Jackie had surpassed their goal.
For all he had endured he was now receiving his reward.
After two years he won the National League batting championship
and Most Valuable Player Award.
He was named to the All-Star team six times
and was the National League MVP in 1949.
Jackie Robinson's breaking of the color barrier in baseball paved the
way for other Black players to join the major leagues.
He also led the way for racial integration into other areas of
    American life.

While ending baseball segregation,
trips in the south also were challenging the segregation traditions.

After ten years playing in the majors and seeing more Blacks
enter the leagues he retired in 1956.

In 1962 he was elected to the Baseball Hall of Fame.
There have been several movies made about Jackie's life.
In 1997, Major League Baseball retired Robinson's jersey number, 42,
for the entire league.

April 15th is celebrated by baseball as Jackie Robinson Day.
On this day, all players and managers wear the number 42
in honor of Jackie too.
He received many awards. He authored several
simi-autobiographies to account for his life.
After retiring he worked in political jobs, civil rights,
an aide to New York's Governor, Nelson Rockefeller, and business.
In 1962 he was inducted as the first Black into the Baseball Hall
of Fame.

On October 24, 1972, he died of a heart attack in Stanford, Connecticut.
His name is in the history books because of Rickey
decided that the time was right for integration and because Jackie
was very good at what he did.
He focused on his game and not the negativity.

Jackie Robinson
https://www.loc.gov/pictures/resource/highsm.24443/

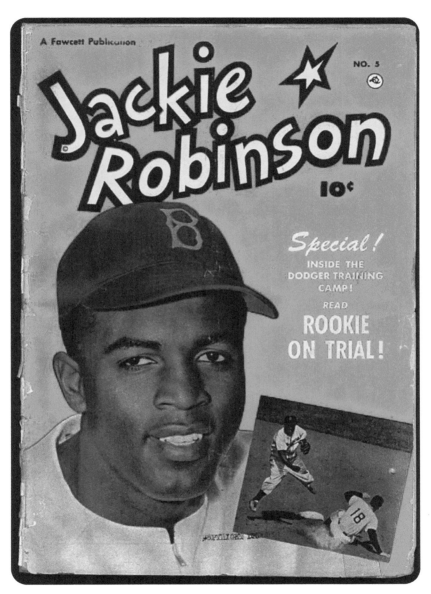

Jackie Robinson
https://www.loc.gov/pictures/resource/ppmsc.00133/

Jackie Robinson
https://tile.loc.gov/storage-services/service/pnp/
ppmsc/00100/00134v.jpg

James "Jessie" Owens (1913 – 1980)

Jessie Owens was born James Cleveland Owens.
He was born in Danville, AL. on September 12, 1913.
His family were sharecroppers. A track and field star not foreseen.
He worked in the fields as a child until they moved
to Cleveland, OH.
In high school he set the world record of 9.4 seconds
in the 100-yard dash.

In 1930 with a job and no scholarship he enrolled
in Ohio State University where his life would unfold.
At 18 in 1931 he married his childhood sweetheart.
She was 16. They had three daughters.
He continued his track and field competitions.

In 1936 he set the world record in the broad jump,
tied his own world record in the 100-yard dash,
set two more world records in the 220yard dash,
and the 220yard dash in low hurdles creating the
greatest single day performance in track and field.
This performance boosted him to join the 1936
World Olympics in Berlin to go against Hitler's pick.

Up for the challenge, he tied the world record for
100yard dash.
In the 200meter dash, he shattered the Olympic record.
He and his teammates won the 400-meter relay.
He broke the record and defeated Hitler's "White Hope"
in the broad jump.
The German competitor displayed good sportsmanship.

He realized that he and Jessie in the same sports had a kind
of kinship.
He congratulated Jessie.
The German leader, Adolph Hitler refused to show good leadership
and make the presentation to Jessie.
Even after Jessie had clearly won the title of the greatest athletic
of track
and field of all time,
and he had even left records for others to climb.

Jessie Owen had earned superstar status in track and field
during the controversy of Adolf Hitler's theory of White Supremacy.
He capturing the hearts of spectators and people of Berlin.

Jessie toured with the team after the Olympics and then returned
to Ohio to graduate with a B.A. in 1937.
Continuing to tour and participate in exhibitions
until he was 39 years old.
At the age of 40 his body grew tired but he never grew tired of his faith
in himself and his country.
He was awarded the Presidential Medal of Freedom.
In 1944 he went to Chicago where he began working with
the youth on the Illinois Youth Commission.
He gave generously of this time.

In 1955 he toured India as a goodwill ambassador for the
United States.
Later he established his own public relations business which he
ran until poor health required him to retire.
He relocated to Tucson, Arizona for warmer weather.
He died March 30, 1980. Flags were flown at half-mask in Arizona.
His body was flown to Chicago for a hero's funeral.

After 1936, Jessie Owen said in a public speech,

"Regardless of color, if a man becomes recognized as an athlete, he has to learn to walk ten feet tall but off the field he has to have his dignity."

"If I can help a young person to be a better person today, then I owe it to him to share my experience.

—*by Jesssie Owen*

Thurgood Marshall (1908 – 1993)

Thurgood Marshall was born in Baltimore, Maryland on July 2, 1908.
His first name was originally Thoroughgood.
He shortened his name to Thurgood in the second grade.
His grandfather was a slave gaining his freedom
by escaping from the South during the Civil War.
Arriving in Baltimore is where he stayed.

Thurgood's father worked as a steward at an all-white country club.
His mother was a kindergarten teacher.

Going to School Thurgood was a good student.
He often got into mischief and was punished for misbehaving.
He became a star of the debate team because he loved arguing.
Thurgood's dad loved going to court and listening to law cases.
Even though his parents had hoped he would pursue a dentist career
like his older brother.
His dad visiting the courts prompted Thurgood to want to become
a lawyer.
He knew the Constitution and how to use it.
Thurgood once had to memorize the U.S. Constitution in high school
as a punishment for misbehaving in class.

Thurgood attended college at Lincoln University in Pennsylvania.
and joined the fraternity Alpha Phi Alpha.
While at college he relished being on the debate team
He also fell in love and was married in 1929.
After graduating from Lincoln, Thurgood aspired to attend
the University of Maryland.
Nevertheless, he was Black so attending there could not be.
Instead, Thurgood went to law school at Howard University.
He finished first in his class in 1933.

After graduating and passing the bar exam, he started a small
law practice in Baltimore.
One of his first large cases was versus the University of Maryland.
Thurgood remembered how they would not admit him because
of his race. He heard furthermore,
in 1935 that another student had been turned away
for no other reason than his race.
Thurgood took the University of Maryland to court and won
the case.
Now they would have to admit Black students into the place.
This was just the start of Thurgood's fight against segregation.

To the NAACP Thurgood began to be known for both his skill
as a lawyer and his passion for civil rights.
He became the chief counsel for the NAACP fights.
Over the next several years, Thurgood traveled the country defending
Blacks who were often wrongly indicted.

He also battled against segregation and the Jim Crow laws
of the South fights.
He eventually received the nickname "Mr. Civil Rights".
In the Brown v. Board of Education, Thurgood's most famous case,
came in 1954.
At that time there were separate schools for
Black children and White children.
It was illegal in many states for Black children to attend
the same schools as Whites.
Thurgood argued that schools should not be segregated, he defended,
the case argument that many states used calling "separate but equal".
Thurgood argued that separate schools could not be equivalent.
For the Civil Rights Movement, Thurgood won in a landmark
case decision.
He showed that it was unconstitutional for schools to
uphold segregation.

He became a Judge in 1961. Thurgood Marshall was appointed as
    a judge
on the United States Court of Appeals by President John F.
    Kennedy.
He served there until 1965 when he became the United States
Solicitor General.
As Solicitor General he represented the federal government before
the Supreme Court.
President Lyndon Johnson nominated Thurgood Marshall for
the Supreme Court in 1966.
He was a great pick.
He was confirmed by the Senate on August 30, 1967
and became the first Black Supreme Court Justice.
While serving on the Supreme Court, Thurgood Marshall
supported the rights of the individual without malice.

He served on the court for 24 years. He retired in 1991.
The replacement of uniqueness of character, debate, and knowledge
difficult to fine one!
He left a legacy of using the law and the Constitution to fight
for all human rights.
He broke down racial barriers, including achieving
one of the highest positions in the government as a member
of the Supreme Court.
While working as a lawyer he argued 32 cases before the Supreme
Court and won 29 of them.
There was a one-man play about the life of Thurgood Marshall
called "Thurgood" which appeared on Broadway starring Laurence
Fishburne in 2008.
Thurgood Marshall died of heart failure on January 24, 1993.

Quotes by Thurgood Marshall:

"Today's Constitution is a realistic document of freedom only because of several corrective amendments. Those amendments speak to a sense of decency and fairness that I and other Blacks cherish."

History teaches that grave threats to liberty often come in times of urgency, when constitutional rights seem too extravagant to endure.

"Certain people have a way of saying things that shake us at the core."

"Even when the words do not seem harsh or offensive, the impact is shattering."

"What we could be experiencing is the intent behind the words."

**Official portraits of the 1976 U.S. Supreme Court:
Justice Thurgood Marshall**
https://tile.loc.gov/storage-services/service/pnp/
ds/11800/11820v.jpg

Dr. Charles Richard Drew (1904 – 1950)

Dr. Charles Drew was born on June 3, 1904, in Washington, D.C.
He grew up in a racially mixed neighborhood of Washington, D.C.
His father worked in the carpet business where he received an
average income and teaching his children the proper doctrine.
Charles was the oldest of four children.
He had two younger sisters and a younger brother.
They all grew up with their mother and father.

In college Dr. Drew developed an interested in medicine.
The McGill Medical School in Canada he attended
because he needed additional classes for Howard to attend.
He later was a professor at Howard.

In medical school Dr. Drew became interested in the qualities
of blood and how blood transfusions worked.
Dr. Drew graduated from medical school in 1933
finishing second in his class for his degree.
Later he did his graduate work at Columbia University
destined to make history.
He became the first Black to earn a Doctor
of Medical Science degree.

He did research in the field of blood transfusions.
improving procedures for blood preservation.
Dr. Drew used his knowledge to create
early in World War II substantial blood banks.

He married a professor in 1939.
They had two children.

He turned out to be the Founding Father of blood plasma
saving many lives in times of trauma.
Dr. Charles Drew was a renowned surgeon, medical scientist,
educator, and had authority on blood conservation.
He was the innovator of blood plasma preservation.
He was an outstanding athlete in football, basketball,
swimming, and track of which he had many recommendations.
He also excelled in academics and received high commendations.

In World War II the United States was suffering heavy casualties.
They could not sustain the huge loss of blood from the arteries.
The government called upon Dr. Drew to introduce its military
blood bank program.
He introduced blood plasma on the battleground without the use
of an angiogram.

It worked so well that he was requested to organize the world's first
mass blood bank project.
He became the American Red Cross Bank's first director.
He received many rewards and honors as one of the world's
prominent physicians.
He was worthy of all recognitions.

He resigned his position with the American Red Cross
after reading notifications from his boss,
the War Department, stating that blood of White donors
should not be mixed with that of Black donors.
He was killed in an automobile accident on April 1, 1950,
when he was injured badly.
He was attending a medical meeting at Tuskegee Institute.
Dr. Drew was always willing to contribute.

The irony of his death is the controversy surrounding it.
Some believe that his life may have been saved
if the nearby white hospital had admitted
him and given him professional medical services he needed.
The nearby hospital was a hospital for Whites and not Blacks.

Quote from Dr. Charles Richard Drew:

> **"Blood from humans only differ by blood groups, not race."**

Dr. Ralph J. Bunche (1904 – 1971)

Dr. Ralph J. Bunche was born in Detroit, Michigan on August 7, 1904.
He had a mother, father, sister, and brother. He was a family of four.
His grandfather was a slave.
His father was a barber,
giving haircuts and shaves.
His mother was an amateur musician.
Pretty common in the day, extended family helped with obligations.

He and his sister were raised by their maternal grandmother
aiding the family whenever.
Money was always insufficient.
He worked helping to obtain his education.
He graduated with honors regardless of his situation.
His academic and athletic talents
provided him with a subsidization.

He attended the University of California in Los Angeles.
He played football, baseball, basketball, and was also a scholar.
He could stand up under pressure.
To add to his athletic scholarship, he worked as a campus janitor.
He did not mine hard work and was not a beggar.
He was not to fail. He was a survivor.
Ralph graduated *summa cum laude* in 1927.
To his family, he was not going to be a burden.

He entered Harvard University with the help of family and
friends.
He was going to make them proud at the end.

He earned his master's degree in government in 1928
at Harvard University. He was appointed a professor
of political science that same year after he graduated.

He married in 1930 and became the father of three.
In 1934 he returned to Harvard to earn his doctorate degree.
In 1936 he published, *A World View of Race*.
The world renown socialist from Sweden was impressed.
He specialized in race relationships.
He hired Ralph as his chief research assistant.
These two great minds created the book,
An American Dilemma which was identified
as the American Blacks study classic.

He was summoned during World War II
to serve in sensitive government positions.
He assisted in laying the foundation for the United Nations.
He helped made the Allied invasion of North Africa a success.
He was the first Black to hold a job for the U.S. Department of State
at a desk.

His diplomatic abilities came to the awareness of world leaders.
He was assigned to the trusteeship of the United Nations.
He became a participant on the Special Committee of the United
     Nations
on Palestine which recommended the partition
into Jewish and Arab states of the nation.
He was a chief mediator.
He was the first Black to be awarded the Nobel Peace Prize in 1950.
He also received awards from many organizations including the
NAACP.

At the age of 58 in 1962 he was fatigued and wanted to retire
but remained on when many petitioned him of their desire.
He received the Medal of Freedom from President
John F. Kennedy in 1963
after adhering to their plea.
He was compelled to resign
as Secretary General of Special Political
Affairs when his health was declining
in October 1971.
He died December 9, 1971.
He was eulogized as the most effective and best known
world-wide political servant.

Quotes by *Dr. Ralph J. Bunche:*

> *"We must fight as a race for everything that makes for a better country and a better world. We are dreaming idiots and trusting fools to do anything less."*
>
> *"There is no problem of human nature which is insoluble."*
>
> *"The United Nations stands for the freedom and equality of all peoples, irrespective of race, religion, or ideology."*
>
> *"The United Nations is our one great hope for a peaceful and free world."*

Dr. Ralph Bunche, Dr. Martin Luther King, Jr., Coretta
Scott King, and others during the Selma to Montgomery,
Alabama in March 1965.
http://hdl.loc.gov/loc.pnp/ppmsca.47934

Dick Rowland (1902 – 1960s?)

(Black Wallstreet – Greenwood District/Tulsa Racial War)

Dick Rowland or Roland (aka "Diamond Dick Rowland", was born in 1902.
His birth name was "*Jimmie Jones*".
It is not really known where he was born.
By 1908 he and two sisters were orphans in Vinita, Oklahoma.
Jones was informally adopted by Damie Ford, a Black woman.
In about 1909 Ford and Jones relocated to Tulsa, Oklahoma.
Jones took Roland as his last name.
His name was recorded as "Rowland."
He gave himself the first name, Dick.
Rowland attended the schools that were segregated.

In downtown Tulsa on Main Street in a white owned
and patronized shine parlor, he took a job shining shoes.
He dropped out of high school.
Tulsa was segregated and **Jim Crow** traditions were strictly enforced.
Black people were not allowed to use white people's toilet facilities.
No facilities for Blacks. Did they think, to hold it were their capabilities?
There was no separate facility for blacks at the shine parlor for Rowland.
The owner had arranged for black employees to use a segregated
"Colored" restroom on the top floor of the building nearby.
When he had to use the restroom, he had to have his customers
to standby.

Tulsa, was a booming oil city, also supported many affluent, educated
and professional Black people.
They treated each other with respect and as equals.

Greenwood was a district in Tulsa which was organized in 1906.
It was established after Booker T. Washington's 1905 tour pick
of **Arkansas, Indian Territory and Oklahoma.**
It was a namesake of the Greenwood District that Washington
had established five years earlier as his own demonstration
in Tuskegee, Alabama.

Greenwood became so prosperous that it came to be known
as "the Negro Wall Street" (now commonly referred to as "the Black
Wall Street").
Most Black people lived together in the district.
Blacks had formed their own businesses for them to benefit.
The created their own services with their own professionals.
They had doctors, dentists, lawyers, and clergy, serving
their peers with all the essentials.

During his trip to Tulsa in 1905, Washington encouraged
    the cooperation,
economic independence, excellence, and the sophistication
they had exhibited.
Greenwood residents selected their own leaders and raised capital to
support economic growth that they advocated.
In the surrounding areas of northeastern Oklahoma, they also
    appreciated
the economic growth that was at a great rate,
the comparative prosperity and participated in the oil boom.
They had anticipations for the district to bloom.

On May 30, 1921, the 19-year-old Dick Rowland, entered the
only elevator
of the nearby building at South Main Street to use the top floor
'colored' restroom.
He encountered Sarah Page, the 17-year-old White elevator
operator on duty.

Rowland going to the "colored" restroom as so many times before
Sarah operated to and from the "colored" restroom elevator door.
They had to know each other by sight at least from before.

Some speculated that the pair might have been interracial lovers.
A dangerous and perhaps deadly taboo and keeping it undercover.
What happened in the elevator is anyone's best guess.
Their stories were never confessed.
A clerk at the clothing store on the first floor,
heard what sounded like a woman's scream.
He saw a young Black man rushing from the scene.
The clerk went to the elevator and found Page disturbed.
Thinking she had been sexually assaulted,
not getting her story, only going on what he suspected.
he summoned the authorities.
Only the clerk's interpretation that Rowland attempted to rape
Sarah was given.
So often in these cases, like others accused falsely by the million.
Many explanations for the incident have been given.
Rowland tripped as he got on to the elevator, the most common.
As he tried to catch his fall, he grabbed onto the arm of Sarah,
who then screamed.
Others suggested that Rowland and Sarah had a lover's quarrel.

Rowland had reason to be fearful.
An accusation alone would put him at risk for hateful
and treatments so dreadful
from attacks by angry mobs of White people.
Realizing the gravity of the situation, Rowland fled.
They would not wait to hear his story but would torture
and kill him instead.
He went to his mother's house in the Greenwood neighborhood.
There he would be understood.

The next morning, on Greenwood Avenue Rowland was found.
He was arrested by a Black patrolman and a White detective.
Rowland was initially taken to the jail the Commissioner had selected.
He said that an anonymous telephone call threatening Rowland's life.
They were willing to do what they could to cut back the strife
to receive a fair trial without hype.
He ordered Rowland's transfer to the more protected jail on the
    top floor
of the Tulsa County Courthouse.
Rowland was well known within the city among attorneys and
    other legal
professionals.
If the mob could get to him, they would be unmerciful.

Many knew him through his work as a shoe shiner.
Some witnesses later reported hearing several attorneys
defend Rowland in their conversations with their expertise
saying that they knew him a long time and that what he was
being accused of was not in him.

With news spreading of the clerk's interpretation, a riot quickly
was incited by whites that lasted 16 hours destructively.
During that time, a white mob started fires and airplanes
apparently dropped firebombs.
The destruction included 35 city blocks by the time it had expired.
Businesses were burned down and 1,256 residences in Tulsa's
prosperous Black neighborhood of Greenwood were rioted and burned.
Everything was destroyed that they had earned.
The destruction resulted in over 800 injuries.
There were 25 Black and 12 Whites(37 dead) confirmed.
The Oklahoma Bureau of Vital Statistics recorded 36 dead officially.
A 2001 state commission examination of events was able to confirm
39 dead, 26 Black and 13 White, based on contemporary autopsies,
death certificates, and other records.
The commission gave several estimates ranging from 75 to 300 dead.

White families who employed Black people in their
homes as live-in cooks and servants were confronted by White rioters.
They demanded the families turn over their workers
to be taken to detention centers around the city.
Many White families complied, but those who refused
were subjected to attacks, vandalism, and were also abused.

As the Tulsa Fire Department crews arrived to put out fires,
they were turned away at gunpoint to allow the fire to expire.
The rioters broke into occupied homes and ordered the citizens
out to the street, where they could be driven or forced to walk
to detention centers.

As many as 6,000 Black residents were interned in large facilities.
About 10,000 Black people were left homeless.
Property damage amounted to more than $1.5 million in real estate and
$750,000 in personal properties.
The loss was equivalent to $32.65 million in 2020.
191 businesses were destroyed, a junior high school, several churches,
and the only hospital in the neighborhood.
Many Black families spent the winter of 1921–1922 in tents as
they worked to rebuild their homes and livelihood.

A group of influential White developers persuaded the city to pass
a fire ordinance that would have prohibited the mass
of Black people from rebuilding in Greenwood.

City planners immediately saw the fire that destroyed homes
and businesses across Greenwood as a fortunate event and incentive.
for advancing their objectives.
Demonstrating   a   total   disregard   for   the   welfare   of   the
        affected residents.
With no thought to atone
they went ahead and made plans to rezone.

The reconstruction committee planned to have the Black landholder
sign over the property to a backstabber.
The properties were then to be turned over to a White appraisal
committee which would pay residents for the land zoned residential
in advance of the rezoning at the lower value zoned industrial
The company would be managed by Black representatives.
on behalf of the city and building commercial would be their prerogative

Their intention was to redevelop Greenwood for more business
use and industrial.
This would force Black people further to the edge of the city
for residences.
At the Oklahoma Supreme Court, the case was litigated and appealed.
The ordinance was ruled as unconstitutional.

For the Black residents most of the promised funding was never raised.
They struggled to rebuild after the riot that destroyed their home and
businesses when they were set ablaze.
The Red Cross asserted their best efforts to assist with Greenwood's
residential area reconstruction.
No one else tried to help them rebuild from the devastation.
With the considerably altered layout of the district and its
surrounding
neighborhoods the rebuilding of the district is not comparable.
The extensive redevelopment of Greenwood by people that were not
affiliated with the neighborhood prior to the riot, also
is proof that the Red Cross relief efforts had restricted success.

Many survivors left Tulsa.
Black and White residents who stayed in the city kept silent
about the terror, violence, and resulting losses for decades largely.
The massacre was largely omitted from local, state and national history.

In 1996, a bipartisan group in the state legislature **authorized the** formation of the Oklahoma Commission to Study the Tulsa Race Riot of 1921.

The city had conspired with the mob of White citizens against Black citizens, stated in the commission's final report published in 2001.

It also recommended to survivors and their descendants a program of reparations.

As a result, to establish scholarships for the descendants of survivors was passed by the state legislation.

It also encouraged the economic development of Greenwood and to develop

a park in memory of the massacre in Tulsa's victims.

The Park was dedicated in 2010.

Schools in Oklahoma have been required to teach students about the massacre since 2002.

In 2020, the massacre officially became a part of the Oklahoma school curriculum.

Later accounts have suggested the number of deaths were under recorded.

The case against Dick Rowland was dismissed in September 1921.

The dismissal followed the receipt of a letter by the County Attorney from Sarah Page.

The police questioned Page but there is no written account of her statement found.

The authorities conducted a low-key investigation rather than launching a

manhunt for Rowland.

The Chief of Detectives attributed the cause of the riots entirely to the newspaper account.

He stated, "If the facts in the story as told to the police had only been printed I do not think there would have been any riot whatsoever."

It is said that an editorial was published that afternoon after

the incident with the clerk's interpretation and gave warning of a potential lynching of Rowland.

It is believed that the paper has apparently been destroyed.

All original copies of that issue and the relevant page is missing from the microfilm **cop**ies.

The Tulsa Race Riot Commission in 1997 offered a reward for a copy of the
editorial but it went unclaimed.

The exact content of the column and whether it existed at all remains in dispute.

The police determined that what happened between the two teenagers was something less than an assault.

Page stated that Rowland had grabbed her arm and nothing more and she did not wish to prosecute the case.

Rowland had left town and no one had ever seen or heard from him.

A total of 27 cases were brought before the court, and the jury indicted more than 85 individuals.

In the end, no one was convicted of charges for the injuries, property damage, or fatalities.

Quotes:

> *"Lurid flames roared and belched and licked their forked tongues into the air. Smoke ascended the sky in thick, black volumes and amid it all, the planes—now a dozen or more in number—still hummed and darted here and there with the agility of natural birds of the air."*

> *"Planes circling in midair: They grew in number and hummed, darted and dipped low. I could hear something like hail falling upon the top* **of my office building. Down East Archer, I saw the old Mid-Way hotel on fire, burning from its top, and then another and another and** *another building began to burn from their top."*

> *—by Tulsa's Victims*

"The sidewalks were literally covered with burning turpentine balls. I knew all too well where they came from, and I knew all too well why every burning building first caught fire from the top."

"Tulsa can only redeem herself from the country-wide shame and humiliation into which she is today plunged by complete restitution and rehabilitation of the destroyed black belt. The rest of the United States must know that the real citizenship of Tulsa weeps at this unspeakable crime and will make good the damage, so far as it can be done, to the last penny."

—Judge J. Martin, a former mayor of Tulsa

Tulsa, Oklahoma (Black Wall Street before the Race War of 1921)
https://www.loc.gov/pictures/resource/npcc.29217/

Black Wall Street after the Race War of 1921
https://www.loc.gov/pictures/resource/anrc.14741/

Refuge Camp after Race War of 1921.
https://www.loc.gov/pictures/resource/anrc.14746/

Greenwood District, Tulsa Oklahoma (Black Wall Street 1921)
https://www.loc.gov/pictures/resource/cph.3a34286/

Garrett A. Morgan (1875 – 1963)

Garrett Morgan was born March 4,1875 in Paris, Kentucky.
He became one of the greatest minds of inventions undoubtedly.
His father was a slave former freed in 1863.
His mother was Indian and Black and the daughter of a Baptist minister.
He also was the son of John Hunt Morgan, a Confederate colonel.

He was the seventh of eleven children.
There had to be a better life than what he was being given.
He left school after the fifth grade and relocated in Cincinnati, Ohio.
Employment search he had to undergo.
He got a job there as a handy man at a sewing machine shop.
From there he soon moved to the top.
His original invention was a belt fastener for the sewing machines.
He later sold the belt fastener for $50.00.
How to make things work more efficiently he was a constant striver.
He was not into sports. He was a brainstormer.

His wife had some experience as a seamstress.
He soon opened a tailoring shop employing 32 employees.
The shop's fine craftmanship demonstrated his expertise.
He manufactured dresses, suits, and coats
even from fur of goats.
In one year, he made enough money to buy his wife a house.
Later they had three sons, he and his spouse.

In 1913 he accidentally invented a hair straightening product.
He marketed the product and succeeded with his G. A. Morgan
Hair Refining Company.

He prospered so much from that discovery that the profits with certainty
allowed him to focus on his other inventions with bravery.

With firemen often being overcome by smoke upon entering burning buildings,
he soon invented the gas mask which he patented in 1944, such a blessing

Masks were not dependable and often would malfunction
leaving lives unsaved and causing firefighters to abandon.
His mask worked so well that they soon were also used
by working men who were exposed to dust or fumes.
Engineers and chemists also started to use them when
dangerous chemicals were in the room.
They were substantially used in World War I on the battlefield
and in future wars.
They were used wherever there were harmful spores.

Garrett later modified his mask to carry its own oxygen.
He founded the National Safety Device Company
working as he envisioned.
He utilized the media to promote his inventions.

During the construction of a tunnel under Lake Erie
The explosion on July 25, 1916, no one could foresee.
The explosion left many men entombed.
Some firemen and policemen were afraid that if they would
go in to rescue them they would also be consumed.
Garrett, one of his brothers, and two volunteers
to rescue them made it their task.
They went in and were able to bring everyone out with the use
of Garrett's masks.

His heroism was published all over the country.
He was given a solid gold medal and the grand prize at the Second
International Exposition of Safety and Sanitation.
The news of his invention and how it saved lives was news
worthy circulation.
He was made an honorary member of the Cleveland Citizens' Group
by the International Association of Fire Engineers.

In 1920 he patented an automatic traffic signal.
With the population growth and vehicle inventions
the thought of happenings on streets would have been dreadful.
It became the precursor of overhead and sidewalk traffic
lights of today.
He sold the invention to General Electric Company for $4,000.
In 1920 he and his colleagues also started a newspaper,
the Cleveland Call, which became the "Cleveland Call and Post"
one of the largest
circulations of Black newspapers in the Midwest.

In 1963 Garrett died at the age of 88 in Cleveland, Ohio
after two years of illness.
He was well known for his business skills and creative mind
that invented the traffic light that brought order and safety
to chaos in the streets and gas masks to improve the safety
of the users amidst unbreathable conditions.

Bill Pickett (1870 – 1932)

Bill Pickett was born on December 5, 1870, in Williamson County,
    Texas.
He was always adventurous.
He was the second of thirteen children to parents who were
    former slaves.
They knew that their son was brave.
He was hired as a ranch hand after finishing fifth grade.
Bill established his skills riding and roping.
Soon the rest he was outshining.
His skills were unique.
Others could not duplicate his technique.
They were highly astonished at his method.
Others probably thought that he was stupid.

He later married and had nine children.
Ranchers or Cowboys, better than Bill, there were none.
After the Civil War when Cowboys became known,
Bill Pickett standing only five feet seven
and weighing about one-hundred forty-five was one of the best.

There was no four-legged animal that he would not undertake.
He was credited with originating the rodeo sport, "Bulldogging".
A style very effective and amazing.
He was nicknamed, "Dusky Demon" for his daring "Bulldogging"
Technique of roping and wrestling steers to the ground.
None like him could be found.
Rumor was that his technique he formed
from watching a bulldog take a ranch steer to the ground.

In 1907, Bill contracted with the 101 Ranch and the Show
Wild West.
He would work with the riders and wranglers who were the best.
Soon Bill became the star of the show.

Bill Pickett was the best and everyone would soon know.
Bill performed for over ten years in the United States, Canada,
Argentina, England, and Mexico
tackling steers to the ground an effectively so.
In 1908, holding on for dear life while being tossed
about like a rag doll, with a steer in Mexico his life he almost lost.
The crowd thought it was an insult, but his boss still won
the bet but at him tossed bottles and stones.

Eight years later in 1916, Bill retired, and a 160-acre ranch he bought.
In 1931, the 101 Ranch was in financial difficulty.
Bill most gratefully
went to his old boss's aide to help him he thought.

One morning while roping horses he was kicked in the head
by a stallion.
Bill Pickett died eleven days later of a fractured skull on April 2, 1932.
He was accredited as one of the greatest cowboys that ever lived.
Bill Pickett was celebrated nationally and internationally as the best
Rodeo performer.
In 1971, Bill Pickett became the first Black cowboy to be admitted
to the National Rodeo Hall of Fame in Oklahoma City.

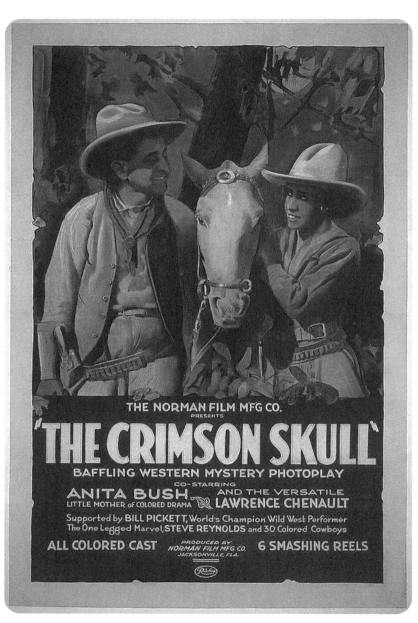

Bill Pickett
https://tile.loc.gov/storage-services/service/pnp/
ppmsc/03700/03759v.jpg

Dr. George Washington Carver (1860 – 1943)

George Washington Carver was born on Moses Carter's plantation
close to Diamond Grove, to slave parents in Missouri.
They had been bought for $700.
For the parents and future children enslaved only minus the
chains and collar.

George was said to have been a frail and sickly child.
His growth was inhibited, and he apparently had impaired vocal cords.
Dr. Carver suffered from repeated chest obstruction and loss of voice.
Some believe that he may have been castration since he was in
the master's house.
They also believe that it was done at the age of 11 years old being
the cause for his underdeveloped vocal cords.
Whoever met him was stunned by his high tone of voice.

A little White boy told him about church, prayer, and Sunday School.
Dr. Carver prayed but he could not go to school or church since
    there were not
any for him.
There was no place to go worship, pray, or sing hymns.
George became a Christian when he was still a young boy,
Vague education early on he obtained.
At age ten he went out on his own to seek his own education
at a high school in Kansas.
As soon as the headmaster saw he was Black to leave he insisted.
Determined, he remained in Kansas.
He worked odd jobs as a cook, laundry helper, and farm hand.
He found a place to live because staying was his plan.

Later he walked to a colored school ten miles away and found a
place to stay.

George never married or had children.
At twenty-five he started Simpson College in Iowa as a freshman.
To follow his education passion he was determined.
After two years, he entered Iowa Agriculture College
now Iowa State University.
While there he did great work in agriculture and botany.
Dr. Carver. testified on many occasions that his faith in Jesus was the only mechanism by which he could pursue and perform the art of science effectively.

Dr. Carver was appointed greenhouse director for his great work
    with soil
and plants and made an assistant instructor of botany.
After receiving his master's, he received a letter from Booker T.
Washington, the head of Tuskegee
Institute asking for instructional assistance.
George went where the southern farmers had been growing cotton for more than 200 years and the soil's minerals were depleted.
Dr. Carver won their acceptance gradually.
He encouraged them to rotate crops to keep the soil enriched.
He persuaded them to plant cloves, peanuts, and peas that replenished the minerals in the soil.
They soon came to realize that for effective crops, it was the rotation and not how much the soil was toiled.

In his lab many tests and experiments were conducted
discovering over two dozen products that could be produced.
Dr. Carver discovered over two-hundred manufactured goods that
    could be
Produced from peanuts and that could be developed from their oils and chemicals.
To be successful usage and demand for new crops had to be introduced.
From the products and industries because of the products
the south economically prospered.

The soil mineral depletion was reduced.

In 1916 George received an honor given to few Americans.

Dr. Carver. was elected a fellow of the Royal Society of Arts, Manufactures and

Commerce of Great Britain.

For years after that award, he received many other great honors.

Dr. Carver spent the rest of his life at Tuskegee doing research, but anywhere

he stood to prosper.

Dr. Carver also spent time on painting, sewing, and knitting his hobbies.

He was held to high esteem all over the world.

Upon returning home one day, George Washington Carver took a bad fall down a flight of stairs.

Dr. Carver was found unconscious by a maid who took him to a hospital.

George Washington Carver died January 5, 1943, at the age of 79 from complications resulting from the fall.

Dr. Carver was buried next to Booker T. Washington at Tuskegee University.

He was very frugal. He had a life's savings totaling $60,000.

George donated it all in his last years and at his death to the Carver Museum and to the George Washington Carver Foundation to provide research for scientist that still exist today.

The farmland where he was born is a national landmark in his honor that his research and contribution benefited all mankind throughout the world.

George Washington Carver was a botanist and agricultural chemist and greatest scientist of all times.

Dr. Carver revitalized the dying agriculture of the 1900s.

When denied education, he went out on his own to get an education.

George Washington Carver was featured on the U.S. 1948

commemorative stamps.

From 1951 to 1954, he was portrayed on the commemorative half dollar coin along with Booker T. Washington.

A second 32¢ stamp honoring George Washington Carver, was issued on February 3,1998 as part of the celebration of the Century stamp sheet series.

In 1977, George Washington Carver was elected to the Hall of Fame for Great Americans.

In 1990, he was inducted into the National Inventors Hall of Fame.

In 1994, Iowa State University awarded George a Doctor of Humane Letters.

In 2000, George Washington Carver was a charter inductee in the USDA Hall of Heroes as the "Father of Chemurgy".

A memorial was erected at Tuskegee in his honor.

George Washington Carver wrote these virtues for his students to live by:

- *Be clean both inside and out.*
- *Neither look up to the rich nor down on the poor.*
- *Lose, if need be, without squealing.*
- *Win without bragging.*
- *Always be considerate of women, children, and older people.*
- **Be too brave to lie.**
- **Be too generous to cheat.**
- **Take your share of the world and let others take theirs**

Quotes by *George Washington Carver:*

On his grave was written, *"He could have added fortune to fame, but caring for neither, he found happiness and honor in being helpful to the world."*

"When you do the common things in life in an uncommon way, you will command the attention of the world."

Dr. Daniel Hale Williams (1856 – 1931)

Daniel Hale Williams was born in 1856 in Pennsylvania.
His dad was a barber. His mother was a housewife.
He was the fifth child.
When Daniel was a child, they went to Wisconsin.
Dr. Daniel inspired to study medicine.
In 1878 he apprenticed under a extremely respected Dr. Henry Palmer.
He mastered the basic which permitted him to go to Chicago Medical
College and received his M.D. in 1883.

Soon his practice in Chicago grew and so did his reputation.
At various Chicago institutes he also earned positions.
Dr. Daniel wanted an institute where Blacks could be trained in a
    variety of
medical professions.
His dream was realized when in 1891, Provident Hospital opened
    with a
biracial staff and nurses' training school.
In the first year with only 12 beds, it served 189 patients.

In 1893 a patient in a brawl was stabbed with what seemed to be
a fatal wound was sent to Provident Hospital.
To save his life Dr. Dan knew he had to be attended to internal.
There was no time to send him out or get anyone else after his visual.
Dr. Dan having to open the patient's chest detected that he had a tear
in his pericardial sac that needed immediate attention.
Dr. Dan sutured the wound. The patient recovered and lived another 20
years proving that the open-heart surgery was a success.
This open-heart surgery had never been done by any doctor
Black or White.

Since he was Black and due to the complexity of the surgical technique, his critics disputed the fact that it was the first genuine surgery. Medical records could not reveal any surgery of its kind being done prior to put to rest the controversies.

In 1894 President Grover Cleveland appointed Dr. Dan as chief
  surgeon
of the largest Black Hospital in the country in Washington
D.C., Freedman's.
His charge for was to reorganize.
This would give him the opportunity to diversify.
He revitalized the hospital by attracting a 20-doctor biracial team
and partitioning the hospital into several specialists including
a nursing school that was his dream.
Dr. Daniel continued to improve the medical profession and
  founded an interracial
medical society in Washington in 1895.
That same year he pioneered the founding of an all-Black National
  Medical
Association to help them to thrive.

Dr. Daniel met and married a schoolteacher in 1998.
They moved back to Chicago after becoming frustrated
with internal politics at Freedman Hospital.
Dr. Daniel returned to Provident Hospital and served on the staff of
St. Luke's Hospital.
He headed one of the largest gynecological departments in Chicago.
Dr. Daniel eventually opened his own practice where the politics he
  could forgo.
He became another first when in 1913 he became the first Black member
of the American College of Surgeons.
Dr. Daniel's personal life although was not happy.
He was left drained by his wife's untimely death in 1924 and other
Family tragedies.

Disillusioned he withdrew into a self-imposed exile and died on August 4,
1931 at his home in Idlewild, Michigan.

He was affectionally known as Dr. Dan.
Dr. Dan was the first doctor, Black or White, to perform an open-heart surgery.
He was known to be willing to serve without pay
in the cause of humanity.
He founded the first Black nurses' training school, at Chicago's Provident Hospital.

Quote by Dr. Daniel Hale Williams:

> *"Anything is possible when it's done in love and everything you can do should be done in love or it will fail."*

Booker T. Washington (1856 – 1915)

Booker T. Washington was born into slavery at some point in 1856.
His father was a white plantation owner. Booker never met him.
His mother gave him the name that the "T" stood for, Taliaferro.
His mother, stepfather, a brother, and a sister worked on
the plantation in Virginia.
They all lived in a small wooden one-room shack.
The children slept on the dirt floor.
Booker had to start laboring for his master when he was about
the age of five.

Booker grew up during the period of the Civil War.
Slavery had left its deep scars.
Although President Lincoln had freed the slaves with the Emancipation
Proclamation, most slaves were not free until the war had over.
In the south no longer having to work for free, they had to move east or
north where they could be paid for their labor.
In 1865, when Booker was around nine years old, Union Soldiers
arrived at the plantation and told his family that they were free.
They had no education, place to live, and no food to eat, you see.
Freedom was great, but Blacks in the South struggled to survive.

Booker's stepfather finally found a job in West Virginia working
in the salt mines.
The family moved there. Booker and his brother got jobs working
in the salt
mines, too. They did not mine.
Booker also worked hard in school growing up.

To get his education, he had to work and go to school but he did not whine.
He learned to read and write at the local school for Black children, but he
also had to work in the mines.

Booker had learned of a college for Black students in Hampton, Virginia
called the Hampton Institute. He wanted his mind to be broaden.
In 1872, Booker decided to leave home and went to Hampton.
It did not stop Booker that Hampton Institute was 500 miles away,
He walked most of the 500 miles, working odd jobs along the way.
He would get rides when possible.

When he arrived, Booker convinced them to let him enroll in the school.
He also took on the job as janitor to help pay his way, still better than
working like a mule.
Booker was smart and soon graduated from the Hampton Institute.
Booker relished school and took a job as a teacher at the Institute.
His attributes were a major positive addition to contribute.
He soon gained the reputation as an excellent teacher.

Booker was recruited to begin a new school for Black students
in Tuskegee, Alabama called the Tuskegee Institute.
When he arrived in 1881 the vocational school did not have any
buildings or school supplies.
It did have plenty of eager students willing to offer physically
and emotionally their expertise. On them he could rely.
At first, Booker was the only instructor, and he taught his classes
in a church.
Booker spent the rest of his life creating the Tuskegee Institute into
a major university.

At first the school was not focused academically.
Students were being taught a trade so they could make a living.
Classes included farming, agriculture, construction, and sewing.
The first students did a lot of the initial work to get the school going
including building school structures and their own food they were
growing.
Booker was proud of all that he and his students had accomplished.
Booker recruited the famous scientist, George Washington Carver, to
come and teach at Tuskegee Institute.
He was married three times and had three children. All of his wives also
played important roles at the Tuskegee Institute.

Booker would travel throughout the south to increase funds and
gain support for the school. He became famous.
He always worked with a plan, not aimless.
With his broad wits, charismatic character, and ethics he could
persuade
or command one to listen, even the skeptics.
Booker also became proficient in communicating and politics.
Soon Booker T. Washington became one of the leaders of the
civil rights movement.
Booker believed in pooling resources and talents.
Booker worked hard to enhance the lives of Blacks in the
United States.
He believed that education, Black owned businesses, and hard work
were the keys to Black successfulness.
He knew for Blacks to be successful could not be achieved aimlessly.
Booker died from heart failure in 1915.
Booker T. Washington was the first Black man on a U.S.
postage stamp.
He wrote a book about his life called, Up from Slavery.
He was the first freed Black man to be invited to the White House.

Quotes by Booker T. Washington:

"Success is to be measured not so much by the position that one has reached in life as by the obstacles which he has overcome."

"No race can prosper till it learns that there is as much dignity in tilling a field as in writing a poem."

"If you want to lift yourself up, lift up someone else."

"One man cannot hold another man down in the ditch without remaining down in the ditch with him."

"Character, not circumstances, makes the man."

Elijah J. McCoy (1843 – 1920)

Elijah McCoy was born in Colchester Ontario, Canada in 1843.
His parents had escaped slavery by the way of the Underground
Railroad to Canada from Kentucky.
Elijah's father worked hard to send him abroad to foster his
educational abilities.
At age 15 he went to Scotland for his studies.

He came back to the United States ready to begin his career
after completing his studies to be an engineer.
He was constantly denied a position in engineering because of his race.
Although well qualified it was always not the place.
Finally, he accepted a position with the Michigan Central Railroad.
The talent he had they did not care to know he was bestowed.
He shoveled coal into the engine and oiled the running parts.
He knew there was a better way from the start.
Elijah was bored with the procedure and soon started to experiment
with a self-lubricating device.
His method was much more precise.

He gained instant fame in the field of mechanical engineering in 1870.
He invented a device that allowed small amount of oil to be dropped
onto moving parts of machines as they were still being operated
awesomely.
Now machines would not have to be brought to a complete stop
to be oiled
by hand periodically.
Elijah McCoy's invention became extremely important to the
industry.
His invention increased business profit considerably.

The labor cost was reduced significantly.

He started the Elijah McCoy Manufacturing Company in Detroit, Michigan.

His invention of the first automatic self-lubricator called "the lubricator cup"

was granted a patent on July 2, 1872.

He had become a mechanical engineer who invented a revolutionary way

to lubricate while they were still being operated the moving parts of machines of the day.

Soon everyone using machines wanted the "real McCoy" signifying quality.

A phrase still used today when they want quality.

For the next twenty-five years he improved and patented more than fifty self-lubricators.

For the quality and efficiency of his inventions there was no duplications.

Later, he specialized in lubricating devices for steam engines and air brakes.

Companies soon learned that what they needed no one else makes.

Elijah McCoy soon started to receive invitations from here and abroad.

When they learned that he was Black, they were quite surprised that such ingenious inventions were conceived by a Black man.

Some would refuse to use the much-needed lubricators for no reason other than because of their racial bias and prejudices!

He would be invited to lecture and be a consultant to large industries.

Not being aware of his race, instead of giving him applaud, sometimes they would cancel his scheduled appearances.

His process is still being used in modern machinery today in automobiles, rockets, locomotives, ships, and many other machines. Elijah McCoy's inventions will always be remembered for modernizing the industrial world.

He died in Detroit in 1929 at the age of 85.

Lt. Col. Allen Allensworth (1842 – 1914)

On April 7, 1842, in Louisville, Kentucky of thirteen children
born into slavery was the youngest, Allen.
Over the years, their family was always separated.
Without family, Allen was always frustrated.
His sister fled to Canada by way of the Underground
Railroad with her future husband with freedom spellbound.

Downriver to plantations the 5 eldest brothers were sold
in the Deep South to cultivate the cotton industry.
His only sibling who was raised in Kentucky
purchased her freedom in 1849 and got married.
They had one son.

His mother was kept by the masters and the mistress
wanting attention for her son one-on-one,
appointed Allen as a young slave to her son.
When the son started school, from him Allen began to learn.
It was illegal and sticking to this rule they were very stern.

Allen's father died when he was younger.
His mother agreed to be sold as a cook to a neighbor.
When Allen was learning to read, he was discovered by the masters.
They separated him from their son and placed him with a Quaker.
Allen could read but it did not upset the new master.
She continued to teach him to read and write.
She also took him to a Sunday school for slave children.
The previous master upon discovering this, took Allen back then.
In 1854 she decided to send him with her husband's partner
to the brother's plantation down the Mississippi River
so that his learning finally would be put to an end.

The boy was placed in the care of a slave steward on the steamboat
for his safe arrival he was to devote.
He was not to be chained with the other slaves below
that were for market sales downriver being transported.

Continuing Allen's studies, the new master had forbidden,
and for trying to do so she beat him.
Allen's new mistress assigned him to be a houseboy.
Also working in the household was a white orphan boy.
The two boys became friends and aided each other to help soften
the times of a cruel overseer on the farm during their sufferings.

In 1855 at the age of 13, Allen intended to flee to Canada.
He spent two weeks hiding on an adjacent farm
without detection or any harm
before going back for his punishment.
Later he ran away again
seeking to be a freeman.
The former and present owners made plans,
to sell him on the auction block.
Allen was sold once more in Memphis, Tennessee
and shipped to New Orleans.

He was purchased, and trained to work as an exercise boy
and jockey in Jefferson, Louisiana.
Discovering that Allen could read, his new master was delighted.
He selected him to run his finest horse and with Allen he was excited.

In early 1861, the Civil War began, but horse racing continued still.
The master took Allen and his horses upriver for the fall meet
    in Louisville.
Allen hoped to see his mother.
After she cared for her last master's dying wife,

he had freed her he had heard.
He discovered that she had recently gone to New Orleans
with a Union man to look for her sons.
In prison she found one.

While working nearby on a farm where he had been left
by his master's deputy,
Allen met soldiers from the 44th Illinois Volunteer Infantry
Regiment, a Union unit which was near Louisville encamped.
When he told them of wanting freedom, they supported
him to join the Hospital Corps. In disguise, he marched
with the unit past his old master through Louisville and off to war.

After some time serving as a nursing aide civilian,
he was invited to go along with one of the surgeons,
to his home in Georgetown, Ohio.
Allen dined with the family of the surgeon
and was given a room of his own.
He felt as if he had first walked as a man free.
The war was continuing. In 1863,
Allen enlisted in the US Navy.
There he earned his first pay as a man free.
He was soon promoted to clerk and Captain's steward.
He served on the gunboats Queen City and Tawah for two years.
He also was putting himself through the Ely Normal School
to improve his career.
Ely Normal was one of several new schools in the South established
by the American Missionary Association.
Allen taught at schools during Reconstruction
for freedmen and their children that were Freedmen›s Bureau operated.
Encouraged by his own instruction,
he began taking courses at the Nashville
Institute but from Nashville he was not graduated.

The school was known later as the Roger Williams University. The school later gave him an honorary Master of Arts degree. Allen became involved with the Baptist Church in Louisville and attended the Fifth Street Baptist Church of Louisville.

He was ordained in 1871 by the Baptists as a preacher. In the 1870s, Allen went to Tennessee to study theology. During that time, he also served as a preacher in Franklin, Tennessee, south of Nashville. In 1875, Allen started working as a teacher in Georgetown, Kentucky. He also served as the financial agent of the General Association of the Colored Baptists in Kentucky. They had joined together to support the founding of a religious school for black teachers and preachers. Allen was among the founders of The State University. Of the president in the early years, he helped guarantee the salary, and served on the Board of Trustees. He returned to Louisville when called to be the pastor of the Harney Street Baptist Church. Upon his arrival, he reorganized and attracted many new members. They renamed the church Centennial Baptist Church. The church was selected as a model by the American Baptist Home Mission Society of America. In a few years, Allen had expanded the congregation almost five times. They also constructed a new church. Allen returned to Kentucky to work and study. In 1868 he joined his brother in St. Louis, where they managed two restaurants. In a brief time, they accepted a beneficial offer and sold them. Allen returned to Louisville.

In 1877 he married. She also was from Kentucky. They had met while he was studying at Roger Williams University in Nashville, Tennessee.

As one of the few Black chaplains in the US Army,
he was appointed by the president and confirmed by the Senate,
as necessary at the time.
His wife was a talented pianist, organist, and music teacher.
They had two daughters together.
He was assigned to the 24th Infantry Regiment,
known as the Buffalo Soldiers.
His family accompanied him on assignments in the West,
ranging from Fort Bayard, New Mexico Territory to Fort Supply,
Indian Territory, and Fort Harrison, near Helena, Montana.
His wife played organ in the fort chapels.

When he returned to Kentucky, he met people from the American
Baptist Publication Society in Philadelphia, who appointed him as
Sunday School Missionary
for the state of Kentucky.
He had always worked to build up the Sunday Schools at his churches,
and this gave him the chance to continue to work on education around
the state.
The Colored Baptist State Sunday School Convention of Kentucky
appointed him to the position of State Sunday School Superintendent.
With his leadership positions and public speaking, Colonel
Allensworth became interested in politics increasingly.
He was selected to the Republican National Conventions as Kentucky's
only black delegate in 1880 and 1884.

In 1886, when he was 44, Colonel Allen Allensworth gained support
by both southern and northern politicians for appointment as
a chaplain in the US Army.
He went to Boston to give a series of lectures after his studies
in Philadelphia in public speaking.
Colonel Allensworth was called to the State Street Church in
Bowling Green, Kentucky.
He also gave public lecture series.

At Fort Bayard, Allen wrote *Outline of Course of Study*, and
the *Rules Governing Post Schools of Ft. Bayard, N.M.*
The Army adapted these for use as the standard manual
on the education of enlisted personnel.
He served in the US Army for 20 years, retiring in 1906.
By the time of his retirement in 1906, Colonel Allen
Allensworth had been promoted to the rank of, Lieutenant Colonel,
the first Black American to gain that rank.
After the army, Lieutenant Colonel Allen Allensworth and his family
settled in Los Angeles.
He was inspired by the idea of creating a self-sufficient, all-Black
California community
where Blacks could live free of the racial discrimination that pervaded
post-Reconstruction America.
His dream was to build a community where Black people might live
and create "sentiment favorable to intellectual and industrial liberty."

In 1908, he founded Allensworth in Tulare County, about thirty miles
north of Bakersfield, in the heart of the San Joaquin Valley.
The Black settlers of Allensworth built homes, laid out streets,
and built public buildings.
They established a church, and organized an orchestra, a glee club,
and a brass band.
The Allensworth colony became a member of the county school district,
the regional library system, and a voting precinct.
Residents elected the first Black Justice of the Peace
in post-Mexican California.

In 1914, the *California Eagle* reported that the Allensworth community
consisted of 900 acres of deeded land worth more than $112,500.
Allensworth soon developed as a town, not just a colony.
Among the social and educational organizations that flourished
during
its best times were the Campfire Girls, the Owl Club, the Girls'

Glee Club, and the Children's Savings Association, for the town's
younger residents, while adults participated in the Sewing Circle,
the Whist Club, the Debating Society, and the Theater Club.
The Girls' Glee Club was modeled after the Jubilee Singers
of Fisk University, who had toured internationally.
They were the community's pride and joy.
All the streets in the town were named after notable Black Americans
and/or   White   abolitionists,   such   as   Sojourner   Truth,
Frederick Douglass,
poet Paul Laurence Dunbar, and Harriet Beecher Stowe, an abolitionist
and author of *Uncle Tom's Cabin*.

Lieutenant Colonel Allen Allensworth was an admirer of the Black
Educator, Booker T. Washington, the founding president and
longtime leader of the Institute in Alabama, Tuskegee
He dreamed that Allensworth could be a self-sufficient community
and become known as the "Tuskegee of the West".

The drinking water was undrinkable suddenly.
The water level fell and became contaminated by arsenic suspiciously.
The dry and dusty soil made farming difficult.
1914 also brought several other obstacles to the town much like
an insult.
First, much of the town's economic base was lost when the Santa Fe
Railroad moved its rail stop from Allensworth to Alpaugh.
On September 14, 1914, during a trip to Monrovia, California,
Lieutenant Colonel Allen Allensworth was crossing the street
when he was struck and killed by a motorcycle.

The town still refused to die. The downtown area is now preserved
as Colonel Allensworth State Historic Park and thousands of visitors
come from all over to take part in the special events held at the park
during the year. The area outside the state park is also still occupied.
Allensworth is the only California community to be founded, financed,

and governed by Black Americans.

The forefathers were dedicated to advancing the financial and social Status of Black Americans.

Circumstances, including a drop in the area's water table, caused the town's deterioration.

After a prolonged fight, the state has preserved the site and is gradually restoring its buildings.

The most important building is the schoolhouse, representing the future of its children.

In use until 1972, it is furnished as on a school day in 1915 as it would have been.

The Park arranges special events to celebrate the former history of the community.

Col. Allensworth's residence is preserved and furnished in the 1912-period.

It contains items from his life in the military service and his ministry.

An annual re-dedication ceremony reaffirms the vision of the original innovators.

A small display of farm equipment is a reminder of the Allensworth economic cultivators.

A public monument, designed by Ron Husband, has been funded by the City of Monrovia, California.

Quotes by Lieutenant Colonel Allen Allensworth:

> *"If we expect to be given due credit for our efforts and achievements, they must be made where they will stand out distinctively and alone," he said, exhorting the residents to "settle upon the bare desert and cause it to blossom as a rose."*

Lt. Col. Allen Allensworth: Copy of Photo Dr. Minnie Ransom purchased at Allensworth Historical Park.

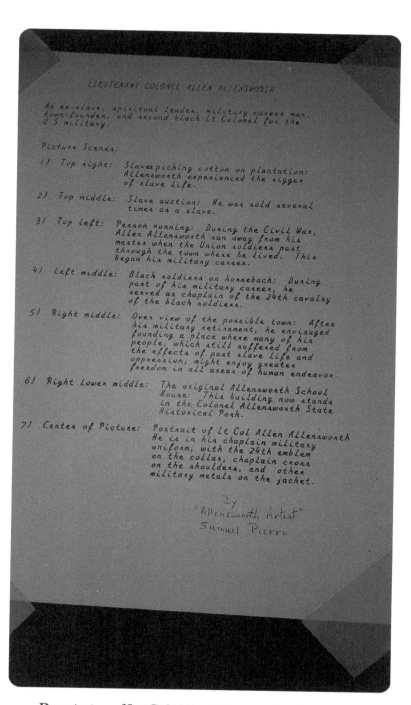

LIEUTENANT COLONEL ALLEN ALLENSWORTH

An ex-slave, spiritual leader, military career man, town-founder, and second black Lt Colonel for the U S military.

Picture Scenes:

1) Top right: Slaves picking cotton on plantation: Allensworth experienced the rigger of slave life.

2) Top middle: Slave auction: He was sold several times as a slave.

3) Top left: Person running: During the Civil War, Allen Allensworth ran away from his master when the Union soldiers past through the town where he lived. This began his military career.

4) Left middle: Black soldiers on horseback: During part of his military career, he served as chaplain of the 24th cavalry of the black soldiers.

5) Right middle: Over view of the possible town: After his military retirement, he envisaged founding a place where many of his people, which still suffered from the effects of past slave life and oppression, might enjoy greater freedom in all areas of human endeavor.

6) Right lower middle: The original Allensworth School House: This building now stands in the Colonel Allensworth State Historical Park.

7) Center of Picture: Portrait of Lt Col Allen Allensworth He is in his chaplain military uniform, with the 24th emblem on the collar, chaplain cross on the shoulders, and other military metals on the jacket.

By
"Allensworth Artist"
Samuel Pierro

Description of Lt. Col. Allen Allensworth photograph.

*Darrin and Sharonda (Dr. Minnie Ransom's son and daughter) in the **Allensworth School** on one of the family's visits to the **Allensworth Historical Park Grant Dr, Earlimart, CA 93219** .*

For this photo, they had a private tour with Mr. Pope who lived in the Colonel's house as a child. He was living adjacent to the property and was also the overseer at the time of their visit.

No one is allowed to sit on the furniture now!

Nat Turner (1800 – 1831)

Nat Turner was born in Southampton County, Virginia on October
   2, 1800
on a plantation.
Nat Turner was recorded as "Nat" in an enslaved nation.
Benjamin Turner, the man who enslaved him and his family
named him actually.
For most of his life, he was called, "Nat".
Slave owners more concerned with labels for property
than names and that was that.
When Benjamin Turner died in 1810, Nat was received as property
to his son, Samuel Turner.
Nat Turner learned how to read and write at a young age.
He was sharp to comprehend and had instinctively intelligent.
He grew up extremely religious in his development.
He would often be seen fasting, engaged in reading
the stories of the Bible or praying.

He often hallucinated which he interpreted as messages from God.
These dreams motivated his life.
Many viewed his as a prophet and non as a fraud.
He escaped slavery at age 21 from his enslaver, Samuel Turner.
In a month after having a vision and developing confusion from hunger
he returned.

In 1824 he had his second vision in the fields under a new owner while
working.
Nat Turner often conducted church services for other enslaved people
and Bible teaching.
Nat Turner also had gained White followers.

By the spring of 1828, Nat Turner was convinced that he was ordained
for a certain great purpose in the hands of the Almighty to be
   his warrior.
He heard a loud noise while working in the fields.
He also heard a voice that told
him that he should take on the fight against the Serpent.
He was confident that God had granted him the job of his servant
to slay his enemies with their own weapons.

On August 21, 1831, Nat Turner took the lead of a rebellion.
Enslaved and freed Black people revolted against Whites that
   persisted
four days for their oppression.
It was one of the bloodiest and most effective in American history.
It provoked a society of fear in Virginia that ultimately
spread to the rest of the South.
It expedited the coming of the Civil War confliction.
Many Southern states, including North Carolina, on Black Americans
tightened their restrictions.

Nat Turner's band of revolutionaries moved progressively in
   Southampton
County from plantation to plantation.
Nat Turner and his allies killed fifty-five white men, women,
   and children.
Over two days, dozens of whites were killed.

In less than twenty-four hours after the revolt began, the rebels
encountered organized opposition and were defeated.
Following this obstacle, Nat Turner and the other rebels struggled to
reconstruct their forces.
The next day, a series of setbacks led to the successful end of the revolt.
Whites reaffirmed their control quickly and brutally.
They killed three dozen Blacks without trials roughly.

Within a few days of the uprising, white organizers became increasingly
confident that the revolt had been restrained and worked to limit the nonlegal killing of Blacks.
Instead, White leaders made sure that the remaining suspected slaves were tried because the White slave owners would be given reimbursement
from the state for convicted slaves.
The state did not give reimbursement to slave owners who owned suspected rebels killed without trials.

Most of the revolutionaries were killed along with countless other Blacks
who were suspected, often without cause, of participating in the conspiracy.
Nat Turner, though, evaded capture for over two months.
He hid in the swamp area and was detected unintentionally
by a hunter on October 30.
Nat Turner surrendered calmly.
Up until his death, Nat Turner believed that it was God's desire for him to
lead the revolution.
On November 11, 1831, at the age of 31, Nat Turner was executed by hanging.

Nat Turner
https://www.loc.gov/pictures/resource/cph.3a39248/

Fredrick Augustus Douglas (1817 – 1895)

Frederick Douglass was born on a plantation in Talbot County,
   Maryland.
He did not know his father. His mother was in slavery.
His birth name was Frederick Bailey.
Working on the plantation was hard daily.
Frederick did not know the exact date of his birth
He later chose February 14 to mark the day of his birth.
Fredrick projected that he was born in 1818.
Life as a slave was very difficult, especially as a child.
At the young age of seven Frederick was delivered to another plantation.
Frederick seldom saw his mother anymore.
She died when he was ten years old. Now he would see her nevermore.
A few years later, he was sent to Baltimore.

Fredrick began learning to read around the age of twelve.
His master's wife began to teach him the alphabet.
It was against the law at that time to teach slaves to read.
When the master found out, he forbids his wife to keep on teaching him.
However, Frederick was an intelligent young man and wanted to learn
to read.
Frederick was intelligent and observant.
Over time, he taught himself to read and write secretly.
He was determined and watched the white children during
their studies frequently.
Once Frederick had learned to read, he read newspapers and other
articles about slavery.
Frederick began to form views on human rights and how people should
be treated.

Frederick also taught other slaves how to read, but this got him into trouble eventually.

He was moved to another farm where he was beaten by the slave owner to break his spirit hopefully.

However, this only strengthened Frederick's resolve to gain his freedom.

Frederick planned his escape carefully.

He disguised himself as a sailor

and carried papers that showed he was a free black seaman.

On September 3, 1838, he boarded a train to the north.

After 24 hours of travel, Fredrick Douglass arrived in New York a free man.

Frederick married his first wife and took the last name, Douglass.

They settled down in New Bedford, Massachusetts.

They had five children.

Frederick was married to his first wife for 44 years before she died.

In Massachusetts, Douglass met with people who were against slavery.

These abolitionists wanted to help abolish slavery.

Frederick began to speak at meetings about his life slavery.

Frederick was a brilliant and articulate speaker that moved people with his story.

He became famous, but this also put him in danger of being captured by his former slave owners and he would be tortured.

Fredrick Douglass traveled to Ireland and Britain to avoid being captured.

Frederick continued to speak to people about slavery.

Frederick wrote his story of slavery in an autobiography called, Narrative of the Life of Frederick Douglass.

The book became a bestseller.

Later, he would write two more stories of his life including My Bondage and My Freedom and Life and Times of Frederick Douglass.

In addition to speaking out for the freedom of slaves, Frederick Douglass
believed in the equal rights of all people.
For women's right to vote,
Frederick was outspoken and provided his support.
He worked with women's rights activists and united with them
for their rights drawing attention
at the first ever women's rights convention
that was held at Seneca Falls, New York in 1848.

During the Civil War, Frederick fought for the rights of Black soldiers.
When the south declared that they would execute or enslave any
captured Black soldiers, Frederick demanded that President Lincoln
counteract.
Finally, President Lincoln cautioned the Confederacy that for every
Union prisoner killed; he would execute a rebel soldier.
Frederick also visited with the U.S. Congress and President Lincoln
insisting on equal pay and treatment of Black soldiers fighting in
the war.
Frederick Douglass died on February 20, 1895, from either a heart
attack
or a stroke.

Frederick Douglass was once nominated for Vice President of the United
States by the Equal Rights Party.
There are many monuments and National Historic Sites named in
his honor.
Frederick worked with President Andrew Johnson about the right
to vote for Blacks.

Quotes by Frederick Douglass:

"A smile or a tear has not nationality; joy and sorrow speak alike to all nations, and they, above all the confusion of tongues, proclaim the brotherhood of man."

"It is easier to build strong children than to repair broken men."

"The life of a nation is secure only while the nation is honest, truthful, and virtuous."

"The life of a nation is secure only while the nation is honest, truthful, and virtuous."

"No man can put a chain about the ankle of his fellow man without at last finding the other end fastened about his own neck".

"Some know the value of education by having it. I know its value by not having it."

Ira Frederick Aldridge (1807 – 1867)

Ira was born on or about July 24, 1807, in New York City.
His father was a straw merchant and a preacher
when he was younger.
His mother died when he was 16.

He went to the New York's African Free School.
Early on he exhibited a fascination with the theater.
Ira enjoyed observing the performers.
Often he was their hidden spectator.
He would peek out from behind the curtains to watch
the action on stage.
Their talents he would gage.

He worked as a steward to get to Europe across the ocean.
The opportunities for a Black man there were more open.
Upon his, he became friends with performers and made connections.
Friends lead him to being allowed to open at a location.
On October 10, 1825, he opened at the Royal Coburg in London.
Ira's first appearance was followed by other performances.
The audience screamed out in terror during his performances.
He won the honor of being one of the greatest actors of the times.

He became an international star with his interpretation
of Shakespeare characters.
Ira's unique style of character engagement continuation
captured the respect of people of all walks of life in Europe.
Royalty also admired his stage presence.

Ira received many honors including the Order of the Chevalier
from the king of Prussia and the Cross of Leopold from the Emperor
of Austria.
He performed personally for the king of Sweden.
Ira also performed for the rulers of Austria, Germany, and
    Czarist Russia.
The Republic of Haiti saluted him as the first man of color in
    the theatre.

Ira married an Englishwoman.
After her death he married again and had three children.
After completing a tour in Lodz, Pollan,
in 1867, he was making plans
to travel around his native land,
America when a serious lung infection
caused him to cancel his plans.
On August 7, 1867, he died at the age of 60.
Howard University's theater in Washington D.C. was named in
    his honor.
His name is also engraved in the Shakespeare Memorial Theater at
Stratford on Avon in England,
in the fourth row with the inscription of the man known as the
    greatest
Shakespearean actor of his time.

Benjamin Banneker(1731 – 1806)

Benjamin Banneker was born on November 9, 1731 in Baltimore County.
Sometime in the late 1600s
a young English servant girl named Molly Welsh
was accused of milk stealing.
In those days when Whites were found breaking the law or cheating
being a servant was often the punishment they were given
and more often than not they would be forced to migrate.
Molly was delivered to America as an indentured servant.
She was without family or parents.

After completing her punishment, Molly purchased a small farm.
She also purchased a couple of slaves to help her work the land.
Owning slaves was the protocol of the day, she thought it was no harm.
She eventually fell in love with one of the slaves named Bannaka.
She later freed the slaves.

Molly and Bannaka had four children.
One of their daughters, Mary, married a freed slave named Robert.
In 1731, Mary and Robert had Benjamin.
Both of his parents were free, so Benjamin was born a freeman.
Benjamin grew up on his family's farm land.
He worked hard even as a child.
and did all sorts of chores around the farm all the while
he helped with the tobacco crops and chopped wood.

Benjamin had few opportunities for school.
Benjamin did attend for a time a small Quaker school.
Benjamin discovered that he had an interest in science and mathematics.

Even when he couldn't attend school, Benjamin borrowed all the books
he could so he could continue learning systematic.
Benjamin became well known in the area as an intelligent young
     man who could
repair machines and work out math problems.

Benjamin's legend persisted after he built his own clock.
Clocks were very uncommon in America at the time.
Benjamin came into contact with a merchant with a watch.
Benjamin made detailed drawings of the internal pieces of the watch
and studied how they worked.
Over several years, Benjamin built a larger version of the watch
out of wood.
He had constructed his own working clock.
Benjamin's clock told the excellent time and worked for more than
forty years before being destroyed in a fire.
His original papers were also destroyed in a fire.

As Benjamin grew older, he began to take interest in the stars.
He read books on astronomy and used math to analyze the movement
of the stars.
Benjamin accurately predicted an eclipse of the sun
before it was done.
After the Revolutionary War, Benjamin began to use his skills
as a surveyor.
Later for his endeavor
Benjamin got a job working on surveying and laying out the new
     capital city
of the United States. Washington, D.C.
Benjamin was appointed by President Washington and served as a
     surveyor
on a six man team helping to design the blueprints with his brainpower
for Washington, D.C., the White House, the U.S. Treasure building,
with grand avenues as they stand today including the Federal buildings.
Benjamin Banneker's helped in selecting the site for the buildings and
in entirety from his photographic memory reproduced the plans

when the chairman abruptly returned to France with the plans.
Thomas Jefferson was an architect but he had drawn up a much smaller
area and plan for the Washington vicinity and much simplier.
It was not anything like the grand area and buildings that still
  exist today.

Benjamin began to publish his famous Almanac in 1792.
The full title was Benjamin Banneker's Pennsylvania, Delaware,
  Maryland,
and Virginia Almanack and Ephemeris.
It included all sorts of information including astronomical data,
  weather
predictions, tables, essays, commentaries, and tide tables.
He published a new almanac each year for six years until 1797.

Benjamin hoped to see an end to slavery. He sent letters to Thomas
Jefferson asking him to consider that all men were created equal,
regardless of race.
He used his almanac as an example
of what a free Black man could accomplish.
Jefferson wrote him back, and agreed that the almanac was
extraordinary,
but he did not do anything to put an end to slavery.
Still to an end of slavery Benhamin waited anxiously.

His life and achievements were used as examples by abolitionists
to demonstrate what a free Black man could accomplish.
Benjamin Banneker wrote a letter to Thomas Jefferson to prove
the perception of "Blacks being infererior to Whites" as being untrue.
Jefferson shared the information with the French Academy
and the Britain's House of Commons to support the education
  of Blacks.

Benjamin didn't see an end to slavery or inequality in his lifetime. He died wrapped in a blanket observing the stars through his telescope on October 9, 1806.

Benjamin Banneker was a self-taught mathematician, outstanding astronomer, an inventer, and author of almanacs.
Many people consider him to be the first Black scientist.
He produced the first wooden clock built in the United States.
He helped in selecting the site for the buildings in Washington D.C. and in entirety from his photographic memory reproduced the plans

when the chairman abruptly returned to France with the plans.
In 1980, a commemorative postage stamp featured Benjamin Banneker Was produced. There are parks, museums, schools, and streets named after Benjamin throughout the United States.

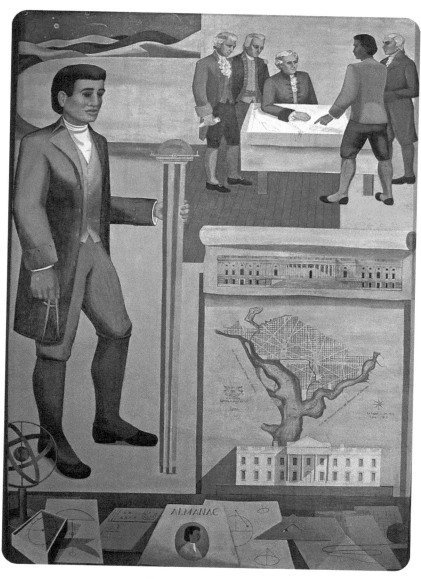

Benjamin Banneker
https://tile.loc.gov/storage-services/service/pnp/
highsm/09900/09905v.jpg

Chase Your Dreams

By: Minnie L. Ransom ED. D.

You are inherently intelligent, creative, and cooperative.
Be the best you, you can be to put you in other's positive perspective.
You have an endurance, survival, and resilient nature
that can be demonstrated without being a bragger.

You have a passion for your goals and will get there.
Take your position or create it to become with hard work and a prayer,
doctors, lawyers, scientists, astronauts, authors, poets,
educators, inventers, innovators, creators, artists, athletes,
actors, or whatever your heart desires.

When given negativity, with all those "You cannot, You should not"
and many other negative put-downs,
keep your eyes on your goals, these may be ways to keep you bound.
These negativities are beneath you, so put them in the ground.
Strip away biases; overcome, go over, or around those barriers.
Keep your focus on your goal fulfillers.

Stand up for what is fair and right.
It does not matter your height.
Have empathy, sympathy, and compassion for others.
In God's eyes, we should treat each other as brothers.
Follow the Golden Rule and treat others as you want to be treated.
Do not be a part of the wicked.

Living in turbulence times, you do not have to be a part of the problem.
Choose to be a part of a relevant solution.

Had a rough experience, be a survivor.
See someone do well, be an applauder.
Help others in any way you can.
It would be nice if everyone made that a plan.
Be a role model that someone can look up to.
Believe it or not, someone is always watching you.

Be honest and truthful instead of a fraud.
Respect yourself and others by your actions no matter the flaws.
Learn to do it and remember getting to the top you do not have to claw.
You say you did not learn it in the past,
you are never too young or old to learn something for generations will last.

Dr. Minnie Ransom and her husband, Joseph
(AKA Papa Joe) on a Bay Cruse with their social group.

Dr. Minnie Ransom and her husband, Joseph
(AKA Papa Joe) in Seattle, Washington.

Dr. Minnie Ransom, her husband, Joseph
(AKA Papa Joe), their two sons, and their oldest
granddaughter on a family trip in Hawaii.

Dr. Minnie Ransom, her husband, Joseph
(AKA Papa Joe), and oldest granddaughter headed out on
a road trip to Yellow Stone and Mount Rushmore with
some of their RV group members.

Dr. Minnie Ransom's husband, Joseph (AKA Papa Joe and son, Darrin in a BBQ Cook-Off Contest). His passion (cooking & entering local contests) besides watching cooking shows and boxing. He won 1st place in this one and most others that he participated in.

Within the left portion of the image (phone screenshot):

6:26

Darrin Ransom
Happy anniversary to my parents! 48 years!
1 HOUR AGO

Mui Lac and 115 others   34 Comments

Like   Comment   Share

**Dr. Minnie Ransom and her husband, Joseph
(AKA Papa Joe).**

CPSIA information can be obtained
at www.ICGtesting.com
Printed in the USA
BVHW012249230523
664715BV00020B/1117

9 781643 148182